SAINT JOHN
FACTS AND FOLKLORE

Gail

Enjoy + Share

DAVID GOSS

David Goss

Sept 21 2015

NIMBUS
PUBLISHING

Nimbus Publishing Limited
3731 Mackintosh St, Halifax, NS B3K 5A5
(902) 455-4286 nimbus.ca

Printed and bound in Canada

NB1105

Design: Jenn Embree
Unless otherwise noted, all photos have been sourced from the author's collection.

Library and Archives Canada Cataloguing in Publication

Goss, David, author
Saint John facts and folklore / David Goss.
Issued in print and electronic formats.
ISBN 978-1-77108-297-6 (pbk.).--ISBN 978-1-77108-298-3 (pdf)

1. Saint John (N.B.)—Anecdotes. 2. Saint John (N.B.)—Miscellanea. 3. Saint John (N.B.)—Folklore. I. Title.

FC2497.4.G683 2015   971.5'32   C2015-900253-2
                                            C2015-900254-0

Nimbus Publishing acknowledges the financial support for its publishing activities from the Government of Canada through the Canada Book Fund (CBF) and the Canada Council for the Arts, and from the Province of Nova Scotia through Film & Creative Industries Nova Scotia. We are pleased to work in partnership with Film & Creative Industries Nova Scotia to develop and promote our creative industries for the benefit of all Nova Scotians.

This book is dedicated to Catherine and Graeme Somerville in deep respect for their lifelong dedication to the community through their many endeavours that have aided the fields of genealogy and history. Their work will be the background for family discoveries and stories, similar to those in this collection, that future writers will find as fascinating to read and retell as I have. Thanks to you both.

TABLE OF CONTENTS

INTRODUCTION

Nobody knows when stories were first told about people, their deeds (and misdeeds), and various goings-on in the area we now call Saint John. Archeologists tell us that the Mi'kmaq and Maliseet began to dwell in the vicinity of Saint John Harbour at least four thousand years ago, but they presumably hunted and fished up the St. John River, not to mention other streams, for centuries (or more likely, millennia) before that. While those first peoples have left us no written records, their oral tradition is the source of the earliest tales from this region.

Perhaps we will someday find out that Viking explorers, Basque fishermen, and even the Chinese sailors thought by Gavin Menzies to have circumnavigated the world in 1421, were the next people to come upon Saint John. Stranger discoveries have been known to come to light.

Whatever the odds of that happening, we do know that Sieur de Monts led a complement—including Samuel de Champlain, a skilled navigator and mapmaker—to explore the area. They reached the harbour into which our majestic river empties on June 24, 1604, on St.-Jean-Baptiste Day—hence the name St. John. Using this event, we can date written as well as verbal accounts of Saint John in European languages accordingly. (Just for the record: Champlain had sketched a map of the region, published in his *Voyages* in 1613, which indicated the existence of two fair-sized Aboriginal settlements in what we now call west Saint John.)

In 1632, Charles de La Tours's fur-trading post became the first known attempt by the French to establish a permanent presence adjacent to the harbour. French forts and other settlements came and went up and down the river during the next hundred-plus years—a reflection of the wars and various disputes between Europeans bent on colonizing the New World, if not an extension of conflicts back home. Among these, one might note the takeover of a French Fort at Jemseg, one hundred kilometres up the river, in 1764, which began a four-year occupation of Acadia by the Dutch!

In 1758, Colonel Robert Monkton established Fort Frederick as the first permanent English settlement on Saint John Harbour. In 1762 a trading post was opened at Portland Point by some people named Simonds, Hazen, and White. Then, in 1783, the large influx of Loyalists who chose or were forced to leave what had become America following the Revolutionary War showed up, and the communities which became Saint John were formally founded.

The stories, history, and facts in this book span a time frame beginning with an indigenous legend about the "Ug-Wug," and continue to the present day. Apart from alluding to this one, however, I'm not going to tell you what any of these involve. That might spoil the fun you're going to have as you come across these yourself.

John Geffken
Researcher

THE PLACE

S aint John is a city shaped by the sea. It was first mapped by Samuel de Champlain on June 24, 1604, when he was exploring the Bay of Fundy looking for a suitable place to spend the winter. While he chose to settle on an island in the St. Croix River, another day's sail westward down the coast, he named the river that flowed into the bay through the Reversing Falls after St. John the Baptist, whose feast day it was. That name was later given to the area that became the City of Saint John with the influx of Loyalists in 1783.

Prior to that, the only settlers were French who arrived with Charles de La Tour, who first came to the area in 1610, and the pre-Loyalist Simonds, Hazen, and White settlers from Massachusetts in 1763. Both groups chose to settle on what is known today as Portland Point.

Charles de La Tour was in Saint John primarily as a fur trader, and chose the location as he could trade easily with the aboriginal peoples who used the river and bay for travel. In

1631, de La Tour established the fort at Portland Point, and in 1640 he sent to France for a wife, and Françoise-Marie Jacquelin came to marry him, sight unseen, at the fort. However, a dispute arose with Charles de Menou d'Aulnay, who also claimed the fort. The de La Tours were driven from the point in 1645. In fact, Lady La Tour died of a broken heart as a result of that skirmish, and that is one of Canada's most poignant early stories. Charles de La Tour eventually married d'Aulnay's widow. He was then 60, she 35, and descendants of the five children born of this union are still found among the province's Acadian population to this day.

When today's visitors are told this story of widow d'Aulnay and widower La Tour's marriage of convenience, they think it is a tall tale. Though it may have been a marriage of convenience, the couple lived in Fort La Tour until La Tour's death in 1666. No one knows what happened to the only child born to Jacquelin at the fort.

Simonds, Hazen, and White—from Massachusetts—were the next settlers and chose the same point, again for its convenience. They prospered in carrying out lumbering and liming operations in the harbour and up the St. John River. They, too, have numerous descendants in the province, and in addition their names are perpetuated in the city to this day in the nomenclature of streets and buildings.

The first English child was born in Saint John on the night the Quintons arrived with the Massachusetts settlers on August 28, 1762.

It is believed 15,000 Loyalists came to Saint John, about half in the spring of 1783 and the other half in the fall of the same year. The harbour they sailed into and the surrounding hills they were assigned as land holdings were certainly known to the British. In 1763 settlers had come to the area from the US when it was under British control. It was not land that was easily worked. In fact, the Loyalists considered Saint John too rocky and too swampy for farming, the skill almost half of them brought to the new lands. Nevertheless, some stayed, but the new city seemed to be jinxed from the start. Only one year after development began around the Market Slip area, it burned down and had to be rebuilt. Major fires in 1837 and 1877 also devastated the downtown of the new city, while lesser fires wiped out chunks of Indiantown in 1899 and the piers of Carleton in 1931.

THE WAR OF 1812

The War of 1812 was a prosperous period for Saint John, as many of the merchants benefitted from privateering activity against American shipping. Some 1,200 ships were captured in the three-year war, and many ships, with their cargo, were towed to Saint John and sold, resulting in huge profits for those who financed the legal pirates of the day. Ships were needed, of course, to engage the enemy, and Saint Johners built them. This prosperity also resulted in the building of one of the most enduring structures on the city's horizon, the Martello Tower.

EARLY SHIPBUILDING

 Saint John continued to build ships following the war, but it was not until 1851 that fame became attached to Saint John–built ships. It was in this year that James Smith built the *Marco Polo* on the banks of the Marsh Creek. Designed as a lumber ship, it was converted in England to a passenger vessel, and was the first ship to sail to Australia and back in under six months. This led to a flurry of shipbuilding in the homeport of Saint John, and the sale of ships and the lumber they carried made for a booming economy. Sadly, that ended with the era of the wooden ships, and Saint John yards did not adapt to the steel and steam era.

The dry dock on Bayside Drive changed all that in October 1923, when it opened what was called the "Biggest Dry Dock in the World" by the newspapers of the day.

BY THE NUMBERS

The dry dock operated successfully for 79 years until it closed in 2002.

In that time, it built 126 vessels.

At its peak, the dock employed as many as 4,000 men and women.

The closing of the dry dock came at a time when the port was also seeing diminished activity. Both had thrived due to the advantages the sea and harbour had long given to Saint John.

Though the harbour is no longer the defining characteristic of the city, it is still an important part of what makes Saint John a great place to live. One of the best ways to experience that is to walk the Harbour Passage, a semicircle of burgundy pathways that hugs the shore of the harbour.

DID YOU KNOW?

A scaled-down version of the *Marco Polo* has been built by tradespeople and volunteers under the direction of community animator Barry Odgen over the past twenty years. Unfortunately neither the port nor the city have agreed to a location on the waterfront where the completed ship can be put on display.

COFFIN SHIPS

 After the Loyalists, the next wave of immigrants to Saint John were the Irish, who arrived some thirty-thousand-strong from the famine-raged country beginning in 1847. They came in "coffin ships," named for their cramped conditions, and many did not survive the voyage. Most of those who remained healthy moved on to other areas of North America, but those who stayed turned their hands to the work that was available. Such building projects included:

- The first Provincial Lunatic Asylum, in 1848, on a hill at the mouth of the St. John.
- The first bridge over the Reversing Falls in 1853.
- The magnificent Cathedral of the Immaculate Conception on Waterloo Street, nearing completion in 1855.
- Laying water lines thorough the city.
- The development that led to the beautification of King's Square.
- Rebuilding the city after the Great Fire of 1877, this time in brick and stone so there would be no further great conflagrations to set the city back.

Mayor Sylvester Earle worked tirelessly to rebuild his city following the great fire of June 20, 1877. His reward? He was voted out of office in the next annual election because it was said he neglected rebuilding the port facilities.

BUSINESS ON THE ST. JOHN RIVER

It was the deep ice-free harbour and its connection to the St. John River that made it possible to float lumber to the city and transfer goods arriving from overseas to inland destinations, the key to prosperity for Saint John in its first century of existence.

Saint John was made the official winter port of Canada in 1899, having, unlike Halifax, connections to both national railways. However, a combination of growth in the west, the political decisions to build the seaway in the late 1950s, containerization, and changes in trade patterns, has diminished the city's importance as a port. Thus attention, to a great degree, turned away from the harbour and its environs, which had made Saint John such a desirable place to live and work in its first fifteen decades.

By 1889, through amalgamation with the north end of the city, known as Portland, the city's population reached 24,200, making Saint John's the fourth-highest population in Canada. The city's Prince William Street was said to have the highest concentration of banks, investment firms, and insurance operations of any street in Canada. Its architecture reflected the financial stature of the businesses. Today, though, the city's growth has stagnated and Saint John is now 78th out of the top 100 Canadian cities. Prince William Street, in the heart of the uptown, is still considered to have the finest intact collection of Victorian structures in Canada.

As the years passed and the docks became less productive, the city began to change from a strictly blue-collar town to having a more diversified employment base. IT work grew as computer technology changed the way the world works, and due to leadership in this field from Saint John–based NB Tel (now Bell Aliant), the city readily adapted to new ways.

Saint John's first skyscraper was the old post office, built in 1878, and is still standing in its ornamented glory at the corner of Prince William and Princess Streets. It qualifies as it has an iron framework, not load-bearing walls as most buildings in the area have.

DID YOU KNOW?

Saint John still ranks near the top ports in Canada in tonnage with 28 million tonnes annually. This is due to petroleum products moving to and from the huge Irving Refinery, LNG Terminal, and also bulk exports from the potash mills at Sussex. However, it is forest products, containers, and metals for recycling that make up most of the work at the port, and the cruise ship traffic that brings glitter and glamour to the harbour.

CONFEDERATION BUST

Confederation in 1867 was not good for the city. National policies of trade worked against local industries, which, in order to compete, often had to sell out to larger Upper or Western Canadian firms, who, to become more efficient, generally closed their Saint John operations. Victims to these moves included:

- Rankine's Biscuits
- Pender's Nails
- Thomas McAvity and Company (fire hydrant manufacturing)
- Atlantic Sugar Refineries

THE FIRST WORLD WAR

The First World War was a prosperous time for the city, again because of the harbour and its convenience for shipping goods needed for the overseas effort. Following the war, the city was an important transshipment location for the many immigrants who came to North America by ship. This continued up into the early 1960s when air travel became the favoured method of immigration.

Originally, this building at the corner of Water and Princess Streets was Furlong's Liquor Store, and the grapes on the decorative work outside made sure even non-readers knew what Furlong sold. It's a great example of the decorative Victorian-era structures throughout the uptown.

THE DIRTY THIRTIES

The thirties were the Depression years in Saint John as they were everywhere else. Men were put to work to build an airport in Millidgeville, to bush out trails in Tucker Park, which became UNBSJ forty years later, and to improve streetscapes like Straight Shore, which became Chesley Drive when it was again widened in the 1960s as part of urban renewal.

It was during the early Depression period that the Irving family, beginning with Kenneth Colin, came to the city. The first major project he undertook in Saint John was the opening of the Golden Ball Building as a service station and parking garage in 1932. Today, it has been converted to corporate offices for the Irvings, and the fourth generation is dedicated to keeping

This photo was taken from the boardwalk at Market Square and looks toward Long Wharf, with Fort Howe and its Saint John sign in the background.

the city's economy rolling. They own all the area newspapers, Canada's largest refinery, a couple of paper mills and a tissue plant, steel and cement fabrication plants, and, with partners, an LNG terminal, to name a few.

Saint John is Canada's fourth-largest cruise ship destination, behind Vancouver and Victoria on the West Coast, and Halifax on the East. Since ships began visiting in 1989, 960 cruise vessels have come into port. The busiest year was 2008, with 79 cruise ships (though in 2010 the port had the highest volume of passengers in a single year at 205,883 on 76 ships). Approximately 2,064,517 passengers and 825,000 crew members have visited the city in the last 25 years. Mary Jane and Kyle Rensler of Baltimore, Maryland, were the two millionth visitors, on September 23, 2013.

CITY STRUCTURE

Saint John currently has a population of 70,063 (2011) over an area of 315.82 square kilometres. The greater Saint John metropolitan area, which includes the suburbs of Grand Bay–Westfield, Rothesay, and Quispamsis, covers a land area of 3,362.95 square kilometres across the Caledonia Highlands, with a population (2011) of 127,761. As of 2014, this area is represented nationally by MP Rodney Weston. Provincially, members of the legislative assembly are: Saint John East, Glen Savoie; Portland–Simonds, Trevor A. Holder; Saint John Harbour, Ed Doherty; Saint John–Lancaster, Dorothy Shepherd; Kings, Bill Oliver; Quispamsis, Blaine Higgs; Rothesay, Hugh J. Flemming.

The mayor of Saint John is Mel Norton. The city is served by one councillor at large, Shirley McAlary, and eight ward councilors. Ward 1 (West) is Bill Farren and Greg Norton; Ward 2 (Central) is Susan Fullerton and John McKenzie; Ward 3 (South) is Donna Reardon and Shirley Reinhart; and Ward 4 (East) is David Merrithew and Ray Stowbridge.

DID YOU KNOW?

Though Saint John has New Brunswick's highest tax rate at 1.78.50 per thousand; in contrast it has the province's lowest electrical rates. Because Saint John Energy was founded in 1922 with the mandate to provide power at cost, its 36,245 customers pay an average of $140.14 monthly, 10 percent less than those in other cities and towns pay for the same amount of energy.

ATTRACTIONS
On the West Side of the City

Reversing Falls or Reversing Falls Rapids

A top must-see. Here, 9 metres of the Bay of Fundy battle with the 724-kilometre-long St. John River for supremacy. When the river wins, there is a normal rapid to the sea, but when the bay is higher than the river, the rapid reverses. Between the two there is a calm period during which people swim the gorge. Kayakers run the rapids and, until recently, so did a jet boat, and a zip line runs over a portion of them.

The mouth of the St. John River where it flows into Saint John Harbour. The Reversing Falls rapids are thirty meters under the twin bridges that cross the gorge at this point—the narrowest possible place for such structures.

DID YOU KNOW?

The first recorded visitor to the Reversing Falls was Estavan Gomez, who, in 1525, came to the Bay of Fundy in pursuit of codfish. In his quest, he came upon the harbour of Saint John, where he recorded a *Rio de la Buelta* or, translated, "River of the Return." Only one river does this trick...the Reversing Rapids at Reversing Falls.

Wolastaq Park

Saint John's newest park was the former site of Centracare, a psychiatric hospital, from 1848–1896. The roar of the Reversing Falls was thought to be calming to the mental health patients. Owned today by the Irvings, the park features two dozen Albert Deveau chainsaw-carved statues that explore Saint John's history, commerce, and industry.

In 2015, the present 172-metre steel arch spandrel bridge at Reversing Falls will be a century old!

Moosehead Breweries

Unfortunately government regulations prevent getting in for a drink or a look at the production line, but the size of the plant, and how it has taken over a full city block, is amazing to see. The brewery opened in 1867 and can produce up to 1.4 million bottles per day. Moosehead products are sold all over Canada, in 50 US states and 14 countries around the world.

DID YOU KNOW?

It was Willie Nelson drinking a Moosehead beer in a movie that opened the American market to penetration by Moosehead. At the time, Canadian laws would not allow the product to be sold in any Canadian province outside of New Brunswick.

Irving Nature Park

The park features eight kilometres of drivable roads, or, for the more robust, parallel undulating walking trails, that give great views of the Bay of Fundy. The area also has the most rare bird sightings than any other location in Saint John. It is an important stopping point for migrating sandpipers and plovers, and it attracts seldom-seen birds such as the glossy ibis and the yellow-billed cuckoo that have been blown off their usual routes.

The Irving Nature Park has 125,000 visitors annually, which is more than double what the Fundy National Park attracts.

Martello Tower

Built to defend the city during the War of 1812, the tower has never had a shot fired from its 2.5-metre thick limestone walls. At 61 metres above sea level, a great panoramic view of the entire city can be gained from the Second World War–era concrete addition atop the tower.

St. George's Church

The city's oldest church opened in November 1821. A unique octagonal tower with a four-faced mechanical clock dates to 1890, while the hall on the north end dates to 1921. St Georges closed December 31, 2014, and its future is unclear.

Carleton Community Centre

This is the oldest continuously operating public building in the city and dates from 1863. It has been a health centre, police headquarters and lock-up, water and sewage depot, theatre, children's community centre, Legion headquarters, and food bank over the years.

Maintained by Parks Canada, the lower portion of Martello Tower is quarried lime-stone from the 1812-1815 era, while the upper cement portion was added during the Second World War.

City East and North

Irving Refinery

Best viewed at night, the Irving Refinery is like a crystal palace lit up for a big celebration. Built in 1960, it has been the largest refinery in Canada for some time, and produces 300,000 barrels of oil a day, with 90 percent exported to US markets.

The Town of Rothesay

Rothesay is without doubt the prettiest suburban community in the Maritimes, and perhaps all of Canada, with graceful homes, stunning river views, and picturesque trails and side roads.

Rothesay owes its existence to the establishment of a railway station in 1860 to serve the line connecting Saint John and Shediac. This station made it possible for well-to-do Saint Johners to summer in Rothesay, and thus the community grew as a summer colony. Many built lavish homes that have been converted to year-round living. Thus there was a need for a school, and the Rothesay Netherwood Private School was established in 1877. It is still a vibrant part of the community. Rothesay once had a number of industries like shipbuilding and furniture making, but has none today, and a commute to Saint John is necessary for most. The community even turned Walmart away when it tried to establish in the Kennebecasis Valley early in the twenty-first century.

Fernhill Cemetery

Originally called the Rural Cemetery, Fernhill was the city's first planned burial ground. It opened in 1848 and 40,000 people have chosen it as their last resting place with room for 40,000 more. It includes many ornamental stones, three tombs, lots of statues, and dozen and dozens of interesting epitaphs, like writer Stu Trueman's, which reads, "Let me outta here!"

Rockwood Park

Within ten minutes of uptown, Rockwood Park is over 800 hectares and has more circuitous trails than most can walk in a lifetime. The park is home to many amenities, including artificial and natural spring-fed lakes for swimming and limited fishing, a children's playground, camping grounds, an 18-hole golf course, and the Hatheway Pavilion (with its Labour Museum) on the shores of Lily Lake, with kayak rentals in summer, skating in winter, and Lily's Café to enjoy year-round.

Saint John Central or, as Saint Johners call it, Uptown Saint John

Barbour's General Store

Donated by G. E. Barbours, spice, coffee, and tea merchants, to mark Canada's 100th birthday, this historic building is a flashback to the days before electricity, and showcases the implements people used to do their daily chores.

Barbour's General Store is not originally a Saint John building, but was floated to the city from further up the St. John River, where it served as a general store in Sheffield.

Loyalist House

The house sits high on a rocky bluff today, but when merchant David Daniel Merritt built it in 1810–1815, the area less than half a kilometre from the harbour was considered wilderness. The Merritts and their descendants lived in the building until the New Brunswick Historical Society bought the house to save it from becoming the site of a service station in 1959. Everything the Merritts ever owned was still in the main house or adjacent carriage house, and the furniture and daily implements in use decades ago have been refurbished for visitors to enjoy to this day. The house has been designated a National Historic Site.

Discover Saint John statistics show that Saint John has 1.5 million visitors annually, and they spend a quarter billion dollars in the area each year.

City Market

Built in 1876, the market survived the Great Fire of June 20, 1877, which destroyed 1,600 structures in the heart of the city. Today its charm is defined by its Georgian window line and upside-down roofline, along with a range of stalls and shops with top-of-the-line local goods for sale.

DID YOU KNOW?

In 1947, Saint John would have sold the City Market to the Metropolitan Stores and it would have been razed, had it not been protected forever by a Royal Charter given to the city by King George III. The legislature could not pass a bill to sell it to private concerns.

Trinity Church

Another architectural gem, the Trinity Church is in the Early English Gothic style with light catching the Kempe and Clayton and Bell stained-glass windows. The chief secular attraction is the Hanoverian coat of arms that hung on the walls of the State House in Boston until Loyalists leaving the area thought it should have a home in their new land and brought it to the city. It miraculously survived the Great Fire and several attempts by the City of Boston to have it returned to them.

Many misjudge the size of the gold-glazed salmon atop Trinity's sixty-four-metre tower. Guesses up to six metres are not uncommon, though it is just two.

King's Square

The focal point of the square is the one-of-a-kind two-tiered bandstand in the very centre of the park. Not to be missed are the flower beds in summer, and a chance to say hello to Sir Samuel Leonard Tilley, in statue form, who gave the nation its name, Dominion of Canada, at Confederation in 1867.

Imperial Theatre

The Imperial Theatre is considered one of Canada's most outstanding theatres both from a decorative and acoustic point of view. Built in 1913, the Keith Albee concern of New York, which said it would never "build in the sticks," was convinced to do so by Walter Golding. Saint Johners have been delighted with the decision ever since.

An August 2013 night of discovery held by Loyalist City Paranormal seemed to confirm that reports of ghosts in the Imperial have some basis. A video of their exploration is worth viewing on the group's website.

The Imperial marked its one hundredth birthday in 2013, and is little changed from this postcard image popular when the theatre was built.

DID YOU KNOW?

Brunswick Square's neighbour, the fourteen-storey Brunswick House at the foot of King, was the city's first modern skyscraper. It was built in 1966 under the direction of German immigrant Hans W. Klohn, who, with K. C. Irving, formed Ocean Steel in 1955.

Harbour Passage

Kilometre one of Harbour Passage begins at the Cruise Ship terminals on Water Street, and currently runs to Reversing Falls without a break, which is about an hour's walk for most people in reasonable shape. There are no facilities along the way, so go before you go!

Saint John Jewish Historical Museum

This museum is the only one of its kind in Atlantic Canada and celebrates Saint John's vibrant Jewish community. The congregation dates back to the 1850s, and at its peak had about a thousand members, though less than one hundred remain today.

Lloyd Goldsmith was elected as the first and only Jewish president of the Saint John Board of Trade in 1979, and was sworn in by the city's first and only Jewish mayor, Samuel Davis.

Old Burial Grounds

RIP Of the 14,000 graves in this 1.6-hectare cemetery, only about 200 stones remain readable. The most interesting is that of Christopher Billop, which details his life in New Brunswick after emigrating from Staten Island with the Loyalists. However, it does not tell the whole story: his ghost reputedly still haunts his original home in New York.

THE PEOPLE

THE SAINT JOHN MAN WHO COULD
HAVE BEEN A SULTAN

"Saint John men abroad have in many instances made a name for themselves, but none of them, so far as local history records, have become rulers in foreign lands." Not just rulers, but sultans, as an article in the *Saint John Daily Sun* of October 25, 1904, noted. Arthur E. Anderson had the opportunity to become the sultan of an island in the Philippines, ruling over several villages and having some hundreds of wives at his beckon.

If it sounds too good to be true all these years later, it sounded the same way to Mr. Anderson in 1904, and he turned down the offer because, as he explained while on a visit to his parents in Saint John, to take the position he would have to "remain for the rest of his life on the island given him." In an interview as he left Saint John, Anderson said he would be returning to Manila where he worked for the United States government as an architect. His friends expressed relief that he had turned down what was obviously a great offer with "strong inducements," and were relieved, no doubt, that he would be back to visit them and his parents in Saint John.

MARGARET ANGLIN, THE GREATEST ACTRESS OF HER AGE, HAD SAINT JOHN CONNECTIONS

Called "the greatest actress of her age" by the *Oxford Companion to the Theatre*, Margaret Anglin was considered a Saint Johner even though she was not born in Saint John, nor did she die in the city. Perhaps her first claim to fame was being the only child ever born in the Parliament Buildings in Ottawa. Although she died in Toronto, giving Ontario more claim to her than New Brunswick, she was the only of Timothy and Ellen Anglin's ten children born outside of Saint John. Anglin herself overlooked the fact that her mother just happened to be with her father, the Speaker in the House of Commons, on April 3, 1876, when she came into this world. Her childhood was largely spent in the family home atop Vinegar Hill on Waterloo Street, and her father divided his time between Ottawa and Saint John, as besides his parliamentary duties he was also the editor of the *Saint John Freeman*. The house Margaret knew as home and the paper her father founded and edited still exist.

Memories of Margaret's glory years on the American stage are all second-hand these days, as her theatrical performances began in 1894 and started to peter out in the mid-1930s, though she performed and taught until just a few years before her death in 1958. Her life is detailed thoroughly in John LeVay's 1989 biography, *Margaret Anglin: A Stage Life.* In this book we learn that Margaret's first stage performance took place when she was six years old, not far from her Waterloo Street home, at the Convent School's Christmas Concert. She played the role of Santa Claus and in her speech told of the "wonders of the North Pole and the advantages of being good for goodness sake." A young Anglin also performed in the city at the Carleton Street Mechanics' Institute and at the Union Street Opera House.

In 1883, the Anglin family left Saint John and moved to Toronto. Subsequently, Margaret moved to New York in 1893 and got her first break in August 1894, playing at the New York Academy of Music in Charles Forman's *Shenandoah.*

Saint Johners were kept abreast of her stage successes. Surprisingly only two years after her initial stage role, the very lively but short-lived *St. John Progress* had an interview with Miss Anglin.

It seems that it was 1912 before Saint Johners got to see her perform professionally in the city, though it is possible she may have visited for personal or performing reasons before that date. Her 1912 visit is well documented in the *Daily Telegraph,* though, surprisingly, not noted at all in the *Saint John Globe.* The occasion was during a cross-continent forty-two week tour of the play *Green Stockings,* which she had helped rewrite from an English play titled *Colonel Smith.* The *Telegraph* headline the day before her arrival read: "Miss Anglin Here Tomorrow. The Famous Actress with Her Entire Party to Arrive on the C.P.R. at 12:40 Noon. Suites Reserved at Royal and Dufferin–Gallery Sale Begins Monday Morning at Nine O'clock, Cast of Characters..."

The main portion of the article began by noting Anglin was nearing the end of what had been "the most successful tour in her brilliant career." LeVay's account notes that she had proudly said after visiting her three home towns of Ottawa, where she was born; Saint John, where she grew up; and Toronto, where she had lived and would end her days, that clear profits were $77,000, a veritable bonanza in those days.

Successful as it might have been, the Saint John visit was not without incident. Anglin wrote a letter to the editor of the *Telegraph* saying, "It has been brought to my notice that I have been unfortunately misrepresented by the newspapers of St. John as saying on the occasion of a former visit many years ago when I was quite a young girl that when I came again the people of St. John would 'pay dearly for the privilege of hearing me.' Both the basis of that article and the tenor of it, I believe to be rather cruelly unjustified. I feel that I must entirely absolve myself from the implication and say that in the present engagement I had nothing to do with the prices charged....The opportunity to play here gave me a great deal of happiness and I accepted it totally unaware of the schedule of prices until I arrived yesterday morning too late to move in the matter and utterly unable under the terms of my agreement to make any alteration in it. I have been deeply touched by the evidences of affection and regard which have been shown me in my old home and if my acting is a source of any pleasure to St. John I hope greatly I may be afforded to be allowed to come again and give it my best."

Nowhere in the coverage of her visits does in mention the price range of the presentation. The review of her work was flattering, and the settings described as "rich in effect and adequately realistic," while Anglin was referred to as wearing costumes that "displayed her beautiful figure to the utmost advantage."

At the close of the show, she retired to the Royal Hotel, and was serenaded from the street by the City Cornet Band, who played, among others numbers, "When you and I were young, Maggie." She, in turn, presented bouquets to the bandsmen.

Then it was off to Halifax, and her career was to continue for many decades to come. Did she ever return to Saint John? Her biography does not say so, but then, it does not follow her every move, so it's possible. Perhaps her last solid connection with the city was in December of 1948, when a Saint John Drama Group was about to enter the Dominion Drama Festival, and manager Stanley Daley sent Anglin a telegram in Toronto asking if his group might be called "The Anglin Players." He was cordially granted permission to do just that.

HANGED AND BURNED IN EFFIGY

Saint Johners seem to have a habit of burning those they dislike in effigy.

Benedict Arnold was no more popular in the city during the six years he lived there (1785–1791) than he had been south of the border. He was considered arrogant and heavy-handed in his business dealings. After he successfully sued Munson Hoyt for slandering his name, the citizens let him know how displeased they were with the judge's decision by burning a straw effigy of Arnold outside of his well-furnished home on the corner or King and Canterbury Streets. Arnold was not long leaving the city for England after that.

In 1830 Sir Charles Edward Poulett Thompson (Lord Sydenham) was burned in effigy in King's Square for the prominent role he played in removing the duty from Baltic timber, thus lowering its price and making it harder for New Brunswick timber to compete. Hundreds of tar barrels were piled around a forty-foot pole in the square (then rough and undeveloped), and on the top, stuffed with gunpowder, was the hapless figure of Sir Poulett. Accounts say that when the fire reached the effigy it exploded, to the delight of the crowd. Later, Sir Poulett became Governor General of Canada, and visited Saint John as part of his viceregal duties. The reception was in the County Court House, within view of where the burning had taken place; indeed, he was escorted to the spot and shown where his effigy had been burned eleven years earlier.

President McKinley was the next to offend Saint Johners. One of the commercial ventures on which Saint John was founded was the quarrying of lime and its sale to east coast cities like Boston and New York, which were growing by leaps and bounds in the late eighteenth century. McKinley thought Maine lime producers should have the market, so he placed a heavy duty on Canadian lime in 1890. Saint Johners hung McKinley at Market Square and lit him afire to show their displeasure with his tactics. It's unlikely McKinley ever knew about the incident, which was related in 1954 in a speech given by W. Gordon Taylor, owner of Snowflake Lime, one of the surviving companies nearly killed by the tariff.

Tom Siddon, the federal Minister of Fisheries, suffered this fate more recently. On June 7, 1989, he was hung in effigy at the end of a wharf on Saint John West's Riverview Drive as eleven local salmon fishers protested the extension of a five-year ban on catching the king of fish in the Saint John Harbour. A sign under Siddon's dangling feet read, "Siddon the Dictator," and another read, "If no answer from you, we are going fishing salmon." However, the hanging made no impression on Siddon, or the Department of Fisheries, who said the men would not be compensated for the extended ban, and if they fished they would be fined or lose the licenses they held but could not use. There has been no commercial salmon fishing in the harbour since, though gasperaux, herring, mackerel, shad, and lobster are still caught to this day.

ROBERT FOULIS, AN INVENTIVE SCOT

Robert Foulis is the famed inventor of the foghorn, which first aided mariners after its installation on Partridge Island in 1859. A century and a bit later, a limerick contest was held to mark the Canadian Centennial and an entry from Dwight Stewart reflecting on Foulis was judged best overall in Saint John. It read:

Robert Foulis said with a smirk,
Ships can't see the shore through this mirk,
From this problem was born,
The world's first foghorn,
Many lives have been saved through his work.

MGM FOUNDER HAD
SAINT JOHN ROOTS

Louis B. Mayer, the Saint John–raised movie magnate and "M" in MGM, was honoured by the city he grew up in on May 19, 1939, when he was made a Freeman of the City. At that time, he asked the Shaarei Zedek congregation if he could remove his mother's remains from the Shaarei Zedek Cemetery (adjacent to Fernhill) to the cemetery in Los Angeles where his father was buried, but was refused permission. As far as is known, he never returned to Saint John after that rebuttal.

DID YOU KNOW?

In 1849, two English men, John and Joseph Bardsley, arrived in Saint John from Bristol, England, and began manufacturing silk toppers and beaver hats for the ship-owning gentry and timber barons of the city. The last of the family members to offer custom-made hats in Saint John were Robert and John, with the shop located at 211 Union Street. The business closed in 1976 but a branch of the company is still in business in Australia, and a Bardsley Hat may be ordered from down under.

DR. BAYARD: SKILLED PHYSICIAN
WELL AHEAD OF HIS TIME

Dr. Bayard lived a long and useful life as one of Saint John's preeminent physicians following his graduation from Edinburg University in 1837, and was still visiting patients until two months before his death at the age of 93 in 1907. At that time he was considered the oldest living graduate of his alma mater in the world.

He is remembered as the founder of the first General Public Hospital in Saint John, in 1860. Even before that he was deeply involved in innovative medical procedures. Twenty-three-year-old Robert Tweedie had suffered from an eye injury since a youth, and over time the eye had enlarged and protruded from the socket, creating such pain that Tweedie eventually suffered from insanity. He was constantly moaning and muttering, was unable to sleep, and refused to speak about his condition. He was placed under the care of Dr. Waddell at the newly built asylum at Reversing Falls, but when there was no improvement in his case, he was referred to Dr. Bayard for surgical attention. Bayard decided to operate, and upon removing the eye from the socket, discovered "a small sac adhering to the case of the tumor, containing a calcareous [ie. containing carbontate] concentration which pressed upon the optic nerve at its exit from the brain."

This was removed, and the patient put to bed, where he raved and muttered for a few days but gradually improved and was released from hospital. Dr. Bayard was delighted the next month to receive a letter from the young man, who had moved to his father's farm at Kouchibouguac, stating, "The eye is perfectly healed...my intellect and tongue came also...the case has astonished all in whom it is known." He signed the letter, as he well might have in the circumstances, "your very grateful and humble servant, Robert Tweedie."

JAMES BRIGGS: "SHOT BY SOME RUTHLESS ASSASSIN"

Though badly neglected over the years, the Church of England cemetery on Thorne Avenue has some interesting stones that tell the story of those buried there. The most poignant story on stones is found on the three-metre, spire-like marker of James Briggs. It reads:

Erected by members of
Portland Division #7
Sons of Temperance
In memory of
their much respected
and lamented brother
James Briggs Jr. R.S.
Aged 21 years
Who was shot by some
ruthless assassin as he
was passing the Long
Wharf, Portland, on his way
home from the Division Room
On the night of the
6th Sept 1847.

The story was carried in all the local and out-of-town papers, and described as a "melancholy incident," "another shocking murder," and "an unprovoked and blood thirsty murder." The cause was ill feeling between the English and the Irish at the time. At the inquest, between forty and fifty witnesses were heard. No one had a clear picture of what happened, and most testimonies seemed to have been coloured by the beliefs of the witnesses, not by what they did or didn't see. In the end, after the jury deliberated for a fortnight, Dennis McGovern was charged with wilful murder. The judge deemed the trial was to take place the following November or January, but no record of this can be found.

The last hanging in Saint John was that of Clifford Edward Ayles, who was hanged outside the old jail on King Street East on November 6, 1956. The hanging was Ayles's punishment for the murder of Alison Graves, stabbed sixteen times during a robbery in Saint John East on October 20, 1955.

BRUCE HOLDER JR. REMEMBERS THE SAINT JOHN SYMPHONY RADIO BROADCAST OF CHRISTMAS DAY 1951

 Under the direction of Dr. Kelsey Jones, the first Symphony orchestra that Saint John ever knew, formed in the fall of 1950. The predecessor of the current New Brunswick Symphony had improved to the point that it was to be featured on Christmas Day 1951 over radio station CHSJ. A news release stated that the radio station had spent many hours taping the orchestra's concerts in order to "discover the most effective arrangement of microphones" and "to study technical problems involved in obtaining proper balance." So, not only were the musicians to be congratulated for their acumen with the instruments and scores, but the radio station technicians deserved praise too.

The concert was to be forty-five minutes in duration, and the highlight was a piece Jones himself had written for the fifty-two-piece orchestra. It was titled "Music for Christmas," and was described by the media as a "deft and sympathetic arrangement of five of the most loved carols." Jones elaborated, saying, "scored for a full symphony, it was written to feature each section of the orchestra playing alone in certain passages."

Bruce Holder Jr. was playing trumpet in that orchestra...he's still playing today! He recalled the piece Jones wrote, and said, "He wrote it so that it seemed like something had gone wrong... the music didn't stop, but it just seemed like there was a problem. At that point, the trumpet section jumped up as if to save the day, and we played a very short jazzy version of *Jingle Bells*.

Dah dah dah, dah dah dah, dah dah dah dah da...not much, but it seemed as if we'd rescued the piece from falling apart, which is what he wanted, though it didn't seem to the audience that was supposed to have happened," Holder laughed.

He also clarified what wasn't clear in the newspaper account. "It was not a live broadcast. We wouldn't have fit into their studio," he laughed. "We did it at the high school. They taped it, and we were home enjoying the symphony on Christmas Day like everyone else."

FOUNDER OF SALVATION ARMY VISITED SAINT JOHN NOT ONCE, BUT TWICE!

William Booth was a tireless traveller and indefatigable speaker for the Salvation Army and its cause. In his lifetime, 1829–1912, it is estimated he travelled some eight million kilometres and preached sixty thousand sermons. It might be said he was the right man in the right place at the right time to carry out the plan he sincerely believed God had ordained for him, that is, the salvation of all people.

It wasn't an easy task to found a new religious movement in Victorian Britain, and William Booth met much resistance when he began his work in the slums of London in July 1865. Politicians opposed him and the establishment did, too. He was roughed up by the very people he hoped to save...not once, but many, many times.

But the movement flourished under the leadership and tireless devotion of Booth and his wife, Catherine. English immigrants brought Booth's ideas to Toronto in 1882, and Salvationists were soon found all across the county. Booth had more than a passing acquaintance with the work in Saint John, having visited the city on two of the four tours he made to Canada. His first visit was to New Brunswick was October 1, 1894, his second on September 23, 1907. During the 1894 visit, he came to Saint John from Digby, Nova Scotia, and upon arrival spoke at a improvised platform set up at Market Square. The following day, some three thousand came to hear him preach at the St. Andrew's rink.

Upon arrival by train at ten in the evening of September 20, 1907, Booth was met by about one thousand people led by Mayor Sears, who welcomed him to the Loyalist City. In reply Booth said he had "pleasant memories of his former visits here and the satisfaction with which he regarded the work of the Army in Canada." He added that "after a wearisome day on the land after a tedious journey" (he was referring to the ocean voyage, which had been very rough), "I am sure you will not expect a lengthy address from me," then added that he hoped he would see all present at "the meeting tomorrow night, and a great many more on the next Sabbath."

Which is exactly as it happened. On Saturday night he conducted a rousing meeting in the auditorium of the new Army Building, and on Sunday, the Opera House was filled to capacity for morning, afternoon, and evening gatherings, at which he spoke for over an hour on each occasion on the work of the Army, and as conclusion to his talks, said more than once, " I have several new projects...but they are not ready for publication."

These words from a man of almost eighty must have been greatly encouraging to the soldiers in Booth's Saint John Army, as, to this day, they are still doing good work in the community he took the time to visit so long ago.

CHARLOTTE HAINES'S SLIPPER

Children in Saint John have grown up with the story of Charlotte Haines's slipper and how it got stuck in the mud at Market Slip. It has been a staple of Loyalist Day storytelling since the slipper was donated to the museum by the Peters family in 1945, and for years following that, no child visited the museum without being told the story and shown the slipper.

Basically stated, Charlotte was the daughter of John Haines, a patriotic American who forbade her to visit with his brother David and his family, as they were Loyalists. Knowing they were departing for British Colonies (then known as Nova Scotia, but part of which were to become New Brunswick), the next day, Charlotte skipped school and went to see her cousins. Unfortunately, the day passed all too quickly, and she did not arrive back home at her usual time, which roused her dad's suspicions. When questioned, she had to admit her visit to her uncle, so her father declared she was not welcome any longer under his roof. Thus, Charlotte's uncle David had to bring her to Saint John. When disembarking on May 18, 1783, one slipper got stuck in the mud, and the other slipper was eventually tucked away by Charlotte. She married William Peters at seventeen, and they had fifteen children. Their descendants all likely heard the story for generations before the family gave the slipper to the New Brunswick Museum.

Many outside New Brunswick now hear a version of the story too, as in 1998, Janet Lunn did a children's book with artist Brian Deines that retold Charlotte's misadventures in a lively fashion. Simply titled *Charlotte*, it is a hit with children who can relate to the young girl and her desire to have one last visit with her cousins. However, though the slipper is pictured, the story of it being sucked into the mudflats at landing is not told. Perhaps the lack of emphasis on the slipper portion was intentional, for the latest thought by the museum curators based on the style and size of the slipper, and the materials used in its construction, is that the slipper that the Peters family gave indicates it could not have been around in 1783, but is more likely to be Charlotte's slipper as a grown woman in the early 1800s. Nonetheless, the story, being a good one, endures, and its telling gives the present generation a link with children of yesteryear.

DID YOU KNOW?

It is improper to refer to the burial ground on Sydney Street as the Loyalist Burial Ground, as many among the 14,000 buried in the 1.6 hectare site are not Loyalists at all, but early Scottish, Irish, and French immigrants.

JACK THE HUGGER MUGGER

In the fall of 1908, and lasting through the early winter, ladies on Saint John's west side were experiencing frequent hugging attacks from a male who would ambush them from behind bushes or fences, then disappear into the night. It was not a regular occurrence, but happened frequently enough that the nickname Jack the Hugger or the Hugger Mugger, was attached to the perpetrator by the newspapers. At first, the police did not take the matter seriously. In fact, on December 21, they issued a statement saying that "Women may go out now, Jack the Hugger is a myth," and that the reports of women being ambushed and hugged in the area of Union Street were without foundation. However, when the "hugging" continued, the police pursued leads and eventually formed the idea that the perpetrator was likely a crew member of one of the vessels that regularly called at the west side port facilities.

On a mid-January night, a couple walking down Queen Street noted a man crouched in an alley and alerted police, who soon arrived on the scene and gave chase. They followed footprints to No. 3 Shed near Sand Point, but temporarily lost the man. They hung around, and in due time a gent answering the description came into the shed, spoke to the staff on duty there, then boarded the ship tied up to the pier. The police followed and were surprised to find their quarry to be an officer on the ship, not a common seaman as they had suspected. Though the man denied being the so-called "Hugger Mugger," the police were sure they had their man. However, lacking solid proof, they were unable to arrest the individual, but promised the ladies of the community he would be watched carefully if he came ashore on subsequent visits to the city. Since there are no further reports of the work of a "Hugger Mugger" in the community, it would seem the police got their man.

DAVID G. LAIRD: HE HARNESSED HIS CLOCK

 Today, we routinely record television shows, set our thermostats and our lights, and use time-control apparatus for dozens of other reasons. In 1934, when time control seems to have been used for the first time in Saint John, it was big news. The *Evening Times Globe* featured a profile and picture of David G. Laird, the man who first "harnessed his clock." In the photo he appears standing beside a mantelpiece with his clock and the apparatuses it controlled.

He explained that in the morning the clock "released the current to the electric stove at a previous set time," then "a few minutes later, the electric toaster went into action," and then, after another few minutes, the radio came on, "calling him from sleep for breakfast." Its final job was to turn on a light, "giving him illumination to dress." At that point, there were four functions available, but Mr. Laird was looking at increasing that to six. No doubt he did, but there is no further information on the matter so it is not known if he was able to cash in on his innovation or not. His results, he noted, came from just "figgin' with various clocks, adding a gear here, and a gadget there," and he pointed out to the reporter covering his story that he was not an inventor, but a "painter and checker for the CPR."

DID YOU KNOW?

Brian Perry is currently the man behind keeping Saint John's last remaining steeple clock running at Trinity Church, where a public clock has been ticking away since 1810.

UNCLE ALFIE OLAND AS RECALLED BY DEREK OLAND

When perusing papers looking into the past, sometimes an item will just jump off the page demanding my attention. That's what happened when I came across an image of Alfred Oland in the *Evening Times Globe* of July 27, 1931, and a headline which read "Starts Canada Trek with $10 in His Pocket."

Now that would be something to follow up, I thought...local lad to walk across the nation intending to see, as the story said, "many new sights," and to "discover how hard it is to get employment in some of the depression areas." He said he intended to "pick up odd jobs to finance his tour" so he would have the necessary "jack" to keep on going.

Alas, no more could be found to indicate it ever happened. And it likely didn't, according to his nephew Derek Oland. "Alfie was a character, to say the least," Derek said when I contacted him to check out the story. "He was probably having a drink with the local reporter and told him what he planned to do. He was always up to something that was just a bit offbeat. He would do something like that for sure. If he did begin the trip, I'd guess he'd of got dry by the time he got to Edmundston and stopped there for a drink before he ever left New Brunswick. And that would be the end of the journey."

Derek shared one other story that illustrates the foibles of his uncle, who was the son of Phillip Oland, owner of the famed Moosehead Breweries. As Derek remembered it, "Princess Elizabeth and her husband, Philip, made a trip to Saint John, I think it was 1951, and the cavalcade travelled down Main Street, past the brewery, through Simms Corner, and down to the DVA Hospital. My family was gathered in front of the brewery, and the whole of Main street was jammed with people intent on getting a view of the soon-to-be-queen. Well, Alfie would have nothing to do with being just one of the crowd. He somehow got up on the roof of the main office of the brewery, where he'd have a stunning view of the princess and her husband. As they approached, he spotted the Prince in his motor car and began to shout 'Phillip, Phillip.' The Prince looked up to see where the voice was coming from, and by the time he looked back to the crowd, his car was past P. W. Oland, G. B. Oland, and the other Olands waving away to him from their position in front of their huge brewery. Alfie kept calling 'Phillip, Phillip,' and finally his dad looked up to see his son waving frantically as the royal couple moved down the street. Well, P. W. couldn't do much but wave back to his son, Alfie, and so he did. Perhaps not very enthusiastically," Derek said with a chuckle, "as Alfie had been a thorn in his side many times and this incident was just one more."

PRINCE PHILIPPE BURIED IN SAINT JOHN? YES INDEED!

Those visiting St. Joseph's Cemetery on Westmorland Road in Saint John east are often surprised to come across the memorial stone of Prince Philippe de Bourbon, who was buried there in March 1949. Though there is not one English word on the gray granite stone, even the most anglophone Saint Johner has no trouble reading the inscription, and realizing it is an unusual find. The words on the stone read:

S. A. R. Le Prince Philippe
De Bourbon Des Deux-Siciles
Né Le 10 Decembre 1885
À Cannes, France
Mort Le 8 Mars 1949
À Saint John.

Only by consulting the newspapers of 1949 can the rest of the story be discerned. The prince was in the city with his wife,

Here's proof a prince was indeed buried in Saint John at the St. Joseph's Cemetery.

the Princesse de Bourbon, who was on a national speaking tour on behalf of the Women's Canadian Clubs. They had been in the county only two weeks, with the tour beginning in Halifax and continuing on to Saint John, where the Prince took sick and was hospitalized. His wife continued on to Montreal, but when his condition, a combination of pneumonia and a heart ailment, worsened, she returned from Montreal. When he died, she said her tour would be cancelled or postponed.

Once the family had been contacted in France, the decision was made to have the funeral in Saint John. The body was laid out at Fitzpatrick's on Waterloo Street, and taken to the Cathedral of the Immaculate Conception for service. Arrangements were made to have a special choir provide suitable music under the direction of Professor Paul Letendre. The funeral mass was celebrated by Rev F. A. Cronin, while the Bishop of Saint John, with the Most Rev. P. A. Bray, presided at the throne throughout the mass and gave the final absolution at the conclusion of the impressive service. There was a large congregation present, and telegrams of sympathy were received from the governments of France, Spain, Italy, Germany, and the United States.

During the winter months, the body of the prince was entombed at Fernhill and buried at St. Joseph's the following spring, where the monument still attracts attention to this day.

THE MYSTERY OF FERNHILL'S ARMLESS WOMAN

Fernhill Cemetery, in operation since 1848, has many interesting stones marking the final resting place of those who lived in Saint John long ago. One of the most unusual is that of Walker Tisdale, for two reasons. Firstly, etched on this stone is the story of his arrival in Saint John. It reads, "Walker Tisdale, who was born of Loyalist parents after the evacuation of the British on board His Majesty's ship 'Brothers' on passage from New York to this province, and departed this life on the 24th day of November 1857, in the 75th year of his age."

Unlike most other markers in the cemetery, this one is a tall column, and atop the column, say fourteen metres up, stands a woman. Some think she is his wife, Eleanor Tisdale, but there is nothing on the stone to confirm that. Many note she has only one arm, and again, there is nothing by way of explanation about that on the Tisdale monument.

Teegan Scott knows the story, though, and says she learned it from her teacher Dianne O'Keefe while on a field trip to study Fernhill's history. "Long ago, there was a caretaker's cottage at the edge of the woods just behind this cluster of graves. One night the caretaker kept hearing strange noises. He wasn't scared of ghosts, but figured some of the local yahoos were trying to frighten him. The sounds were right around the Tisdale monument. They didn't stop, so he got alarmed, and fired a shot into the air hoping to scare off the noisemaker. It worked, but his shot hit the figure of the lady, and knocked off her arm."

Is there any truth to the story? Ann Maloughney thinks so. She was the long-time manager of Fernhill, and says staff have told the story many times over the years, and it is believed the man who did the shooting was the cemetery's first caretaker, Joshua Clayton.

The story of Fernhill was once the subject of a film short by the National Film Board, which was titled *Boo Hoo*. Unfortunately, all copies have disappeared.

CHARLES M. SHELDON SURE MADE SAINT JOHNERS MAD

One of the enduring Christian fiction classics is Charles M. Sheldon's 1897 book *In His Steps*. It was a big seller when written, and a century later is still selling well (30 million to date!). However, Christians in Saint John can be excused for being a bit annoyed with Sheldon after his visit to the city in 1903, when he spoke to a huge crowd (and read portions of his famed book) at the Victoria Rink. He continued his continent-wide evangelical appearances and, while in Santa Barbara, California, about as far as he could get from Saint John, spoke negatively about what was happening in New Brunswick's biggest city. He used the city as an example of a place that had lost its interest in religious matters, and where, during the summer months, thirty churches had closed their doors and were not holding evening services.

Mr. McInnes, a Presbyterian minister at that session who had intimate knowledge of conditions in the Maritimes from visits to the area, doubted the validity of Sheldon's statement. He got in touch with the Saint John Evangelistic Alliance, who assured him that their churches, though suffering from declining evening visitors in summer, were indeed still open. Sheldon, who said he'd been told of the situation by Saint John clergymen when he visited the city, promised he would correct his statement in future talks. But, as some said at the time, the damage had been done and it would be hard to correct it. Few at the time likely gave much thought to the fact that within a century, Sheldon's comments could be looked upon as prophetic.

GRAEME SOMERVILLE SHARES SOME WESLEYAN CEMETERY STORIES

Alexander McLeod

Alexander McLeod was a Saint Johner who seems to have lived for 160 years, according to his memorial stone in the Wesleyan Burial Ground on Thorne Avenue. Graeme Somerville, who has been involved in the restoration and care of the cemetery for the past 40 years, loves to take folks to the McLeod stone and ask them to determine how long Alexander lived. The dates on the stone are 1773–1933, which, even without a calculator, most quickly figure at 160 years. This startles them, until they are told the story by Somerville. "I am only surmising what happened," Graeme says to them, "but around 1898, Alexander's son came from down south in the US to see where his dad was buried. The original sandstone had weathered badly and could not be read, so he ordered a new granite stone to be placed on the sandstone base. When it was cut, his dad's death date of 1833 was chiselled in as 1933. I doubt his son ever knew the error occurred, as it would have taken a couple months for the work to have been done and by then he was back home. Today, it would be easy to correct the error, and make that 9 into an 8, but we don't think we should change what was done. It's just a bit of a curiosity that we like to point out to those who come to visit."

George Thomson

Hardly a summer passes without Graeme getting a call from visitors who want to be taken to the final resting place of their ancestors, sometimes with interesting results.

Scotsman George Thomson settled in Saint John in 1816, and died in the city in 1841, had a new twist added to his life story in 2007.

Thomson, who built at least 40 vessels, of 539 tons on average, also outfitted a derelict vessel, the *Daedalus*, in 1835 as his living quarters, and it became known as Thomson's Ark. It was the scene of many grand parties and social occasions in its dozen years in Saint John Harbour, secured at Rankine Wharf, near the Fort La Tour site.

Though Thomson's only child left Saint John after her father's death, Thomson's other relatives did not forget him. His monument in the Wesleyan Burial Ground is in the form of a tomb table with six stout stone legs. Over the decades, the one- by two-metre sandstone slab became severely weathered, and much of the lettering became indecipherable. Though there had been a tremendous amount of care given to the existing stones in the cemetery during the last three decades of the twentieth century, Thomson's stone received no special attention.

Then a most unusual event occurred. On June 5, 2007, Graeme Somerville got a call from Susan and John Finch of Roswell, Georgia, who had come to Saint John on a cruise ship and were interested in seeing the grave of David McLellan, also buried at the Wesleyan cemetery. Graeme and his wife, Catherine, took them there and showed them the stone, which Graeme noted was "as easy to read as the day it had been placed there though the sandstone had been blackened by 150 years of seacoast weather."

Standing at the stone, Susan turned to her husband and said, "This is a moment for which I have been waiting for years." From long years of dedicated genealogical research, Graeme knew the relationships of many buried in the cemetery so at that point, he asked Susan if she would like to see another relative. He explained David McLellan's sister-in-law's husband was buried nearby, namely George Thomson. He had married Phoebe Knight, while David had married her sister, Mary Ann Knight. Of course she was interested. More than interested as it turned out. "Out of the blue," Graeme said, "Susann asked 'Could I replace the monument?' She added, 'If I don't do it, it will not get done.'

After checking with the Trustees of the Burial Ground for permission, approval was granted. Graeme noted that in "addition to paying for the new granite slab for Thomson, and the engraving of same, she left $1,500 to cover the cost of removing the old tomb-table, and preparing the footing for the new monument. After all expenses, there was still $800 left over which was placed in the Perpetual Care Fund for further work on this historic cemetery."In addition, Graeme noted, she funded work on Mary Ann McLellan's marker in Fernhill as Mary Ann had remarried after David had died and was buried there under a stone that needed attention.

It was all very gratifying to Graeme, who had worked tirelessly in caring for the cemetery. He added, as he finished telling the story, "Hopefully, there will be many more who will follow Susan and John's example in looking after their ancestor's gravesites and monuments."

QUEEN VICTORIA HAD TO SETTLE A SAINT JOHN ARGUMENT

St. George's Church on the west side of Saint John is the city's oldest, having offered services since opening on November 6, 1821. However, there was an interruption in the services offered, which makes the claim of longevity questionable. On January 3, 1867, Bishop Medley appointed Reverend William Walker as the incumbent to replace Canon Frederick Coster, who had retired after serving since 1825. Walker was appointed because, in the eyes of

St. George's Church as it appeared when Queen Victoria had to settle an argument on the selection of a minister for the church.

Bishop Medley, St. George's was not "high church" enough. In other words, it did not follow the bishop's leanings toward what was known as the Oxford Movement, or offer an evangelical presence in the community by holding the Eucharist as the principal service of the church.

The Bishop's appointment enraged the congregation, used to forty years of Coster's "low church" methods, and on April 13, 1867, they boarded up the doors and windows of the church, informing the newly appointed rector the church was closed for repairs.

This split the congregation. Those who supported Walker as the new rector went to St. Paul's in the Valley (central Saint John) and witnessed his induction as rector of the parish of Carleton, which was done by Reverend DeVeber. Walker then began to hold services at the Temperance Hall on King Street, just north of St. George's. That summer he began legal proceedings against the corporation treasurer, James Ritchie, claiming Ritchie was withholding funds due to him as rector of the parish.

At the ensuing trial, the jury found that Walker had no claim to the "glebe land revenues" the church collected from properties they owned, as he had not been appointed rector of the parish according to law. Walker, however, was not about to give up. In a subsequent trial, he won a verdict against the church corporation by proving their election at the annual meeting was illegal, as there had been no rector or clergy appointed by the bishop present. Walker was awarded damages of one cent!

The newspapers had a field day with the matter which "thoroughly sickened the public," according to one comment made at the time.

The battle raged on for four years until the problem was sent to Queen Victoria for adjudication. The Queen was titular head of the church then, as her descendant is now, though it would be unusual for either of them to be called to make the type of judgment she was asked to in this case.

Exactly who brought the case before her is not known. Her judgment, though, was that Walker was indeed the rector of the parish of Carleton, and its church, St George's. By then it was 1871, and the doors had been locked on the church for four years. In the spring, the barriers were removed and Walker took to the pulpit. However, it was short lived. In April he preached his last sermon and announced his resignation. He took a parish in Yonkers, New York, as his next charge.

How Rev. Walker made out there is unknown, but one thing is for sure: Queen Victoria would have had no influence in any decision made in the USA.

Thus, some would say St. George's four-year closure should be deducted from the 1821–2013 record, and this would make St. John's (Stone) Church, which opened in 1824, the city's oldest continuously operating church. At the time of publication, the future of St. George's is in question.

The only authorized copy of the famous British artist DeCarlo's painting of a boy scout in the company of Jesus, titled *The Pathfinder*, is in historic St. George's Church. The painting is dedicated to Stanley Olive who, though in his sixties, founded the Scout troop there in 1925.

SAM HOWARD AND THE ARGONAUTS SWIM CLUB

Long-distance swimming competitions seem a thing of the past in Saint John today, but in the 1920s and '30s they were one of the stellar summer activities in the bay and on the river. Among those who hung around the shoreline of the city were Sam Howard, Art Quigg, Dave McManus, and Eddie O'Toole, four of perhaps a dozen men known collectively as the Argonauts Swim Club. They dominated the local swimming scene. But despite many feats of endurance and the winning of numerous competitions, both locally and in Nova Scotia, they are not in the New Brunswick Hall of Fame nor the Saint John Hall of Fame. That is not for lack of trying on the part of Carol Harris, who knows the story through her uncle Sam Howard. In her own words, Carol related one of the stories of the first swim ever attempted through the Reversing Falls in the summer of 1930. "Art, Dave, and Eddie began well, but along

Same Howard, champion long-distance swimmer, and the car that he and his partners used to travel to swim meets all over the Maritimes. Carol Raynes

the way, Art and Dave were swept in an eddy pool. Eddie held up until his two friends were safely out of their dangerous position. All three finished the race with Dave first, Art second, and Eddie—who could have won had he not be concerned for his friends's welfare—last."

Though Carol's uncle was the holder of many trophies for his long-distance swimming in the freezing waters off McLaren's beach and his relay races with the other men on the St. John River (they swam the 136 kilometres from Fredericton to Saint John in relay fashion), he was not in that historic Falls swim. Carol believes it was because her uncle had "sustained a badly injured ankle in a fall from the cofferdam" which was then under construction at what was become the Navy Island terminal at the mouth of Saint John Harbour. "These men were not just sports-men, they were working men," Carol pointed out. "Though my uncle survived the fall from the cofferdam, his career as a swimmer did not."

These days, the exploits of the Argonauts live on only in dusty trophies, yellowed newspaper accounts, and a few photographs of their activities. With competitions relegated to the indoor pools of the area where there is no danger of being swept out to sea by the tides, or of being caught in the swirling whirlpools in the Reversing Falls, it is not likely there will ever be another Argonauts club to draw thousands of Saint Johners to the falls.

DID YOU KNOW?

On November 16, 2013, Carol Harris married child-hood sweetheart George Raynes, both eighty-three at the time. The nuptials made the national news on CBC, and the Saint John couple was featured in *People* magazine.

INTERESTING AREAS
AND INCIDENTS

A COUP FOR THE *EVENING TIMES GLOBE*

Charles Dickens's *The Life of Our Lord*, written for his children's delight and edification in 1849, was a "precious family secret" until it was released for public enjoyment in March of 1934. The *Daily Mail* of London, England, had purchased first world serial rights from Dickens's son, Henry, for $210,000, and the *Evening Times Globe* subsequently secured New Brunswick first publication rights, though the sum paid was not disclosed. The paper announced on March 1 that the 14,000-word creation would be published in daily portions beginning on March 5. Were Dickens alive, he would have been shocked to know that his effort at telling the Christian story for his children was being sold at $15 a word. (Even today, authors receive about 50 cents a word for most general magazine work.) The paper's announcement drew praise from local clergy, from school board officials, and known authors like H. A. Cody, who said, "Anything from the pen of Dickens must be good." Readers of the story in the *Times Globe* were encouraged to cut out the well-illustrated daily offerings and bind them into "first edition" scrapbooks, as "with Easter close at hand," the clipped story would make an "appropriate gift to a friend here or in another land." To help fill the scrapbooks, the *Globe* printed a facsimile of the first page of Dickens's original script in his own handwriting.

The *Times Globe* ceased publication on November 23, 2001, leaving Saint John with just one daily paper, the *Telegraph Journal*, which circulates about 30,000 copies through the province.

BATHING WASN'T AN EASY TASK IN EARLY SAINT JOHN

We take it for granted today and enjoy a bath or shower daily, but this hasn't always been the case. In 1838, the city opened a water line at the centre of King's Square. Water did not come into the home, but was available only at established city centre locations and had to be carried home by the pailful. So, a sponge bath was the way most used to clean up.

Even before this, in 1836, an enterprising American named Tilbe created a solution and established public baths at the foot of Britain Street. When he left town on business, the baths were under the care of G. C. Newington, who advertised on July 9 that with the help of Mrs. Tilbe, the "warm baths will be in readiness night and day." By the 1850s, not only could one go for a bath, but could have a meal of oysters while there. An advertisement from the *New Brunswick Courier* on June 19, 1853, told the story fully:

> *Pavilion*
> *Bathing and Oyster Saloon*
> *No 3 Cross Street*
> *The subscriber has fitted up the handsomest apartment in the city for the accommodation of the public and he also returns his thanks for their kind patronage since his commencement in the present business. The baths are ready from 8 am until 10 pm until further notice*
> *Prices for Bathing*
> *Single Bath   £0. 1 3*
> *Five Tickets   £0. 5 0*
> *Tickets for three months £ 1. 5 0*
> *Yearly Tickets   £ 5. 0 0*
> *Yearly or quarterly customers will have privilege of coming when they please.*
> *N. B. Steam house heating Fixtures will be fitted up if required,*
> *June 19   M. Brady*
> *No. 3 Cross Street.*

For those curious about the location of Cross Street, which does not appear on Saint John maps today, it was located off Middle Street in Saint John West, approximately where the first exit off the Harbour Bridge leads to Market Place West.

BETHEL MOVEMENT FOR NORTH AMERICA BEGAN IN SAINT JOHN

Long before the establishment of the current churches of the same name, the term "Bethel" was revered in Saint John and in seaports around the world. The Bethel movement was a non-conformist approach to sharing the Gospel with seafarers by holding mission services aboard their ships. The idea began in London on June 22, 1814, when Zebedee Rogers had a surprisingly successful service aboard a ship on the Thames. London was the leading port of England, and England the leading Maritime nation at the time. In 1817, Rogers had a vision of a distinctive flag he could fly, known as the Bethel flag. When it was run up the mast of a ship docked in port, seafarers knew a religious service was in progress and could join in. A 1986 booklet on the movement written by Roald Kverndal noted that the first service of this kind took place in North America in 1820 in Saint John, when "Rev Mr. Scott, a Baptist minister from Lyme, Dorsetshire, emigrated there in March of that year." At that time, the city was the most important wintertime sea link to Britain in North America. Scott conducted mission services among the seafarers, some of whom might have been to similar services he'd participated in on the

Thames before he left for British North America. Subsequently, the work moved across all of North America, and it was the precursor of the Seaman's Mission to sailors, which still operates in Saint John and in ports through the world.

CONTROVERSY ON CHIPMAN HILL

 Loyalist lawyer Ward Chipman had a fine home built atop the hill that bears his name, which is an extension of Prince William Street north to Carleton Street in central Saint John.

Chipman House was torn down in the early 1900s and a YMCA established on the site. This was a controversial move as Chipman House had been the home of a leading Loyalist family and many thought it should be preserved as a historic home. The new Y lasted only fifty years—in 1951, a new building was put up on the site. By the end of the century, it was in bad financial shape, and not able to pay its tax bills. In a controversial move, the province bought the property, thus negating the taxes owed to the city, and put up a huge Justice complex that many believed far exceeded the needs of the community. To add to the controversy, when it was scheduled to open, the pipes burst in the new structure, and it was never made clear who paid for the repairs and the inconvenience of the opening date being set back many weeks.

A constant neighbour of the three structures has been the 1904 Saint John Carnegie Library Building, which itself began its life in controversy.

In 1897, a committee was formed to build a library atop Chipman Hill. American philanthropist Andrew Carnegie donated $50,000 for the project, one of 2,800 he financed around the world, but the only one in Atlantic Canada. The committee hired G. Ernest Fairweather to design the building, and called for bids for the 27- by 25-metre (88- x 82-foot) building on a 55- by 27-metre (180- x 90-foot) lot just opposite where the famed lawyer's mansion had stood.

Following a call for bids, the committee accepted the lowest bid, from the well-known firm of John Flood, but since the bid was higher than the committee expected, they decided to revise the work to be done and call it again. Three thousand dollars of work was deleted, and on the second call James Myles was the lowest bidder.

Myles then turned the job over to Alderman Robert Maxwell. Maxwell was not only a member of council, but a member of a committee of council overseeing the construction. Questions about a conflict of interest arose.

When the work fell behind (it was six months late) the *Saint John Globe* asked Mayor Walter W. White if there was a $25 per day penalty for the delay. The mayor admitted there was. The *Globe* pointed out that the public believed the penalty had been waived, but the mayor said that was not the case, although he admitted that no attempt had been made to collect it. In his opinion, the whole matter was "a storm in a teacup." He further stated that there was no scandal, and that the *Globe*'s description of the project proceeding at a "go as you please gait," was not warranted, as the building was now complete.

When the library opened on November 16, 1904, the contractor listed was James Myles and Robert Maxwell was noted only as having done the masonry work. Other firms that were involved included J. E. Wilson, sheet metal; interior woodworking by the Christie Company; painting by G. R. Craigie; heating and plumbing by G. E. Blake, and electrical by Hiram Webb.

Hurd Peters, a city official, was the first to climb the stairs of the new structure. The stairs themselves have become the latest controversy, as the grand granite steps at entry were slated to disappear with the completion of the Justice complex and Peel Plaza projects.

However, due to public pressure, the stairs were not tampered with and still lead to the building foyer, which is now the Saint John Arts Centre. However, few climbing them to enjoy a concert or arts event realize the extent of the controversy that has occurred in and around the old library.

The first link of the city centre pedway system allowing indoor passage from the harbour to the market was built over Chipman Hill at a cost of over a million dollars in 1983.

CELEBRATORY DAYS OF YORE THAT ARE JUST A MEMORY...SOME NOT PLEASANT

We don't celebrate many of the special days our ancestors thought important and marked with great ceremony. In the past, the mayor had the ability to call a public holiday when he deemed it wise to do so, and even a regatta or a few sculling races in the harbour would be cause for a day off. While the business community was not pleased with the idea, they knew right well there would be little business done when such an occasion was held: in this era before legalized lotteries, betting on sports events was about the only way a person could hope to come into a sudden fortune. So everything was bet on, and everyone went to see how a match—be it speed skating, sculling, horse racing, baseball, hockey, curling, or walking competitions, to name some of the sporting attractions that could be bet on in pre-nineteenth century Saint John—would turn out, and more importantly, whether they were on the winning side and could collect on their bet.

Then there were the patriotic days that were marked. Four examples follow, of which most Saint Johners will only remember the third.

Trafalgar Day

Modern-day Saint Johners do not mark Trafalgar Day in memory of the British victory over the French and Spanish during the Battle of Waterloo, on October 21, 1806. It was once a very important holiday in Saint John, with flag raisings, parades, and ox roasts in King's Square. It was such a big thing in the early 1800s that a set of stairs at Market Slip were named the Trafalgar Steps. They led to the ferry to Carleton, or Saint John West as it is known today. A plaque still marks the location, though the steps are long gone, and the ferry service ceased operating at that location in 1838.

Joy Day and Prince Day

Joy Day, which marked the end of the First World War, is also a forgotten celebration of the past. It first occurred on August 14, 1919, and was followed by Prince Day, which paid tribute to a visit from the Prince of Wales. On that day there were parades, band concerts, a fair in St. Andrew's rink, "shows" in all the theatres, and nine churches in the uptown area provided free lunches for soldiers in town for the celebration.

Arbour Day

Another day that has died out is Arbour Day. Yes, trees still get planted, but schools don't beautify their grounds or begin summer gardens as they did a century ago to mark the day. Saint John would have no mature trees if it were not for the Arbour Days of the past. For example, in 1884, the New Brunswick Historical Society oversaw the planting of three hundred trees in Queen Square, which, a news article of the time noted, added to the three hundred they had planted the year before to mark the city's centennial.

The trees planted in 1883 were to honour the Queen, Governor Carleton, Senator John Boyd, Sir Leonard Tilley, and Judge Wilmot. Unfortunately, of the 300 planted, 150 died before the October 1884 ceremony, so we do not know if any of trees left in that park honour the Queen or the men who served New Brunswick in her stead so long ago.

Moving Day

Another day that has disappeared is Moving Day, which was May first. It was never a holiday; in fact, it was a dreaded day on the calendar of those who had to move. For some, it was by choice, as the only way they could keep their rent from being raised was to move to another flat. Landlords had to advise of rent increases in February, giving renters three full months to arrange a move or pay more rent. Estimates vary, but some years as much as 20 percent of the population would be on the move on May first. This meant the truckers and cartmen could gouge the movers, and they took advantage of the situation. There are instances on record of movers stopping mid-move and demanding more money or the

Loyalist Days were the big summer celebration in the 1970s through the mid 1980s, when the DeLancy's Brigade, shown here, could be seen marching through the city.

furniture they were handling would be tossed off the wagon and left at the curb. The practice ended following the Second World War and the introduction of modern government legislation on tenant's rights.

May 18, known as Loyalist Day, marks the city's founding in 1783 and until the recent provincial education department standardization of schedules for school breaks, schoolchildren in Saint John enjoyed an extra holiday as the city marked the occasion.

CRICKET, YOU SAY?

Yes, cricket was a popular sport in Saint John, but it has had its ups and downs over the decades according to George Betts, who may have, during the bicentennial celebration of 1983–1985, played the last game of cricket in the Saint John area. In a newspaper article on May 16, 1984, he outlined the history of this typically English pastime, noting that until 1840, "on each fine summer afternoon after the business of the day was over," cricket was played on the north side of King Square where a fine playground had been prepared. Betts was not there, of course, but based his information on David Russel Jack's Centennial Prize Essay of 1883.

Betts had done some research beyond Jack's statement, and found accounts of lively matches between Saint John, Sussex, Moncton, and Fredericton teams from New Brunswick, and the Garrison and Wanderers Club from Halifax. He discovered there had been a Saint John Cricket Club formed in 1855, and among the players was the inventor of the foghorn, Robert Foulis, and the manager of the famed Paris Crew and sheriff of the City of Saint John, James A. Harding. Of course there were others, as it takes eleven players to field a side. In a photo taken of the May 17, 1984, game on Rothesay Collegiate Field, Betts is shown with nine others, and as he pointed out in his story, most were "expatriate Englishman."

In finishing up his historical account, Betts noted, "By 1890, baseball had already appeared on the New Brunswick scene. This was to prove a severe rival to cricket. Eventually it would eclipse it entirely."

Well not quite, it seems. Betts was not sure at the time if this game would be another of the high points in the story of cricket in the province, and while no revival happened immediately afterwards, Betts would be happy to know that the sport is still played in Fredericton, and a Saint John team is in the process of forming.

EARLY DENTISTRY IN SAINT JOHN

On September 6, 1905, Doctor of Dentistry A. F. McAvenney delivered an essay to the Dental Association of Halifax on the history of dentistry in Saint John. In this he revealed the province's first dental advertisement appeared in the *New Brunswick Courier* on February 8, 1823, by Mr. Rath, "Surgeon Dentist," advising he was moving from the city. He went to Fredericton to practice but returned to Saint John two years later, according to a second advertisement McAvenney found and dated with the aid of Clarence Ward, who had spent a lifetime poring over old Saint John papers and collecting trivia about the city's past. Ward's find revealed that on July 23, 1825, a Boston dentist who came to the city was subject to a Medical Board examination before being allowed to practice, which indicates there must have been a number of dentists practicing, but only one advertised: Mr. Rath.

In 1844, two dentists by the name of Vanbuskirk, with the aid of Dr. Bayard (founder of the Saint John General Hospital), administered ether to a patient for the first time in the city. This was only shortly after Dr. Horace Wells had discovered "surgical anesthesia," McAvenney told the Halifax audience.

In his talk on dentistry, McAvenney made it clear that most of the dentists came to Saint John from the eastern United States, and most, it's also clear, stayed only long enough to hone their skills before moving on to larger centres. Among these was a Dr. Fiske from Salem, Massachusetts, who was the first to make what were called "carved block teeth," using gold plate, in the 1860s.

In 1867, a dentist arrived from Paris, one Louis de Chiverie, whom McAvenney described as "hovering between Halifax and Saint John" for his practice. Chiverie, it was stated, was most known for his "outdoor displays", which was likely work done from the back of a wagon in a public park. He notes that, "no such character has visited us since."

Obviously, McAvenney had not come across, or had chosen to ignore, the exploits of Edgar Parker, the Tynemouth Creek–born and Philadelphia-trained dentist who legally adopted the name of "Painless Parker." Just out of dental school in 1892, he began his practice in New Brunswick in the traditional fashion by opening an office in St. Martins. For his efforts, after ninety days he had taken in only seventy-five cents.

When the Kickapoo Medicine Company came to the village to stage the lively medicine show they used to draw attention to their patent medicine products, Parker was inspired to take his dental practice on the road. He walked forty kilometres to Hampton in September 1892, and staged a flamboyant back-of-a-wagon, three-ring-circus-like "painless promotion" and was soon taking in as much as fifty dollars a day. He staged the show in Saint John, before moving on to attract patrons to his dentist chair across Canada and into America. For years he kept just one step ahead of authorities and dental associations trying to put him out of business.

By the time McAvenney wrote his historical review, Parker had been across North America with his promotional methods, back to New Brunswick on at least two occasions, and then moved his family to Brooklyn where he lived more or less permanently in 1896. That's where he married Frances Elizabeth Wolfe, and where he met promoter Bill Bebee, at which point his practice really took off. This was where some of his most outrageous promotion stunts—a high wire walker outside his office for one—brought droves of customers his way. He eventually had fifteen dentists with forty-five chairs on three floors of the building, and seventeen dental offices in the New York area. By 1906, after ten years in Brooklyn, he was worth about half a million dollars, and ready to retire. He was but thirty-four years of age!

Though dentists at the time would not admit it (ethical dentists of the time did not even advertise!), Parker had revolutionized the practice of dentistry. He was the first to establish a multi-chair dental practice like those common today. He got people thinking for the first time about dental health with his wild schemes. Though they did not recognize him for it, he got patients into the chairs of what were known as "dignified dentists" for attention, too.

DID YOU KNOW?

In January 1847, Saint John saw the first use of ether as an anesthetic to "render insensible a patient" in British North America. Dr. Martin Hunter Peters used it to control pain during an operation on a longshoreman's arm.

FELINE FESTIVAL FLASHBACK: CATS OVERRAN SAINT JOHN WATERFRONT

For International Cat Week in 1956, Jean Sweet dug into back issues of the journal *Acadiensis*, where she found a 1906 account of cats overrunning the central portion of the city in 1836. As the story went, an unnamed city merchant promised a cargo of farm-fresh New Brunswick produce to a Boston concern, who in turn arranged for its sale in Massachusetts. Though they had agreed on a price, local conditions changed and the merchant could not deliver at the price quoted. So "he squirmed out of the deal," as Sweet wrote, and left the Boston man "holding the bag."

The Yankee trader seemed to take it all in stride, but he immediately began to think of ways he could pay back the Saint Johner who had left him in the lurch. Next time he came to the city, he happened to mention that there was a ship's crew in Boston Harbour buying all the cats they could, at five and six dollars each, to transport to one of the West Indies Islands where there had been a terrible invasion of rats.

The Saint John merchant immediately sent out word to all the boys in the community that he would pay sixpence apiece for all the cats they could bring to a warehouse on a wharf in the South End where he was collecting them for transshipment to Boston. For the next few days, the boys rounded up cat after cat and delivered them to the merchant at the shed, which he had sealed to the point the cats could not escape. When he had six hundred felines behind the doors, he got a telegram from Boston saying that, "Unfortunately, the West Indies had been well supplied with cats from the Southern United States," and the Saint John animals would not be needed.

The Saint John man had been paid back, and he still had those cats on his hands. So down to the warehouse he went with two brave men at his side, flung open the doors, and "six hundred angry cats fought their way free and spread throughout the waterfront area," as Sweet described it 120 years later, marking the special week dedicated to cats.

"For days," she added, "it was hardly safe to go near the wharf," and as well, to go near the merchant, whose fury over the incident "was something to see. No one," she concluded, "dared mention the word 'cat' to him as long as he lived."

GENEROSITY PERSONIFIED
A different Irish immigrant's story

 This item offers quite a contrast to the usual story told of the Irish experience aboard vessels, often called "coffin ships" due to the dismal conditions on board, as they crossed the Atlantic to Saint John during the famine years.

A letter of thanks appeared in the *New Brunswick Courier* on October 1, 1847, signed by twelve Irishmen. These men wrote on behalf of the eighty-four passengers on the brig *Caroline*, which had just arrived in Saint John from Limerick. Their thanks was being tendered to Mr. H. Thompson, owner of the vessel, Captain Thomas Honey, and mate Mr. Woods. Mr. Thompson had not only provided for their fare, he had also provisioned the ship with "goods of the best Quality for their use." The captain, for his part, was charged by Mr. Thompson as he left the ship at Shannon, with "paying every attention" to his passengers during the voyage. He did just that and more, giving them live fowls from his own stock, and even providing his own bed for one who had none to lie in. The men wrote that there had not been "one person sick on board" and gave credit to being on "board a good vessel," and having a captain of "profound learning, skilful experience, and exemplary good conduct." They also admired the captain, mate, and crew for being temperate men. The captain, they wrote, "showed himself like a father, went from berth to berth as if they were all his own family, preparing proper food and medicines for us with his own hands."

"Where shall we find words to return thanks for such acts of generosity," they wrote in concluding their letter, "May the God of Mercy prolong his days, and crown his labours with success on every voyage he makes...is the ardent prayer of every passenger on board."

The Saint John location most associated with the Irish is Partridge Island, where the sick were quarantined and some two thousand perished. The island is once more being considered for development as Canada's Ellis Island. Since this proposal has existed since the 1880s, it remains to be seen if this latest attempt with come to fruition.

GOOD FISHING AT THE DRY DOCK?

"Fish, tons of it. Fish, thousands of them." That was the hope of Saint John East residents whenever the dry dock was ready to float out a ship. To do that, the dock would have to be filled with water from the bay, and when the water came in, so did herring, smelt, and other varieties of small fish. Once the vessels were out of the dock and a new one moved in, the pumps would be turned on to remove the water from the dock. On most occasions, a few fish would remain on the dock floor when the pumping was complete. On at least one occasion, in September 1933, there were so many fish that the pumps were plugged. The 240 workers at the dock were given permission to take home what they wanted, and once they had all they could carry away, word got around the community. Mothers sent their boys with wagons to take the free

SAINT JOHN, N.B., DRY DOCK, (LARGEST IN THE WORLD.) CANADA.

The dry dock. When it was flooded to remove ships, the fish came in.

fish home. So the next time there was a flooding everyone was on the watch, hoping for another bumper crop of fish to augment the home larder in what was a very difficult period in the midst of the Depression.

GIANT EAGLE CARRIES OFF NINE-YEAR-OLD BOY IN PISARINCO

While enjoying a last taste of summer in a field at Pisarinco, known as Lorneville today, the nine-year-old son of James Ferguson had no idea he was being seen as supper by a bald eagle soaring on the updrafts over the seaside community. But as the young boy lay staring at some natural wonder, the eagle swooped down, grabbed his coat, and soared into the sky heading for nearby woods, doubtlessly hoping to find a private place to enjoy his meal. Fortunately, the lad proved to be just a bit heavier than the eagle had imagined, and its "ascent was very labored, but steady," as the news report the next day in the *Daily Telegraph* put it. The *Daily Sun* said that the eagle "had not gone far before it tired and slowly settled to the ground." At that point, the boy wisely grabbed firmly onto a fence post, and hung on for dear life. His dog, which had been playing with him in the field, had followed the flight of the eagle and at that point attacked the bird, which returned the "onslaught with great vigor," as the *Telegraph* reported it. With the eagle's attention diverted, the boy took off on the run for home. By then, his father had heard the noise, gathered up his gun, and run to the field with the aim of shooting the bird. However, by the time he got to the spot, the eagle was high in the sky, already looking for his next victim. Several others who witnessed the event claimed the eagle had an almost five-metre wingspan.

Internet sources indicate that the heaviest weight an eagle could pick up would be 2–3 kilograms (4–6 pounds), though an eagle can pick up about half its weight and drag prey along the ground.

HEATED SIDEWALKS
A good idea that went bad

When the provincial government built the five-storey Provincial Building on Charlotte Street in 1959, it tore down five buildings in order to provide off-street parking for staff and clients. Great pains were taken at the time to plan a substantial building that would offer government services in a comfortable and fashionable style. In descriptions of the work, it was mentioned again and again how every effort had been made to use New Brunswick materials and local tradespeople in the construction. One of the more innovative ideas was the placement of underground heating coils in the driveways and parking lots surrounding the building. A press report of the time notes that ten kilometres of underground piping was being laid, in which nine thousand metres of heating coil would be placed to circulate five thousand litres of a 50/50 antifreeze and water solution. This, the news report noted, would automatically take care of the snow removal problem.

Though the piping was carefully tested before being covered with three inches of concrete, and then further sealed with two and a half inches of asphalt, it did not stand the test of time. In fact, if you go there today, you'll see the same snow removal equipment on the grounds as you would see anywhere else following a storm. Though it could not be confirmed, it seems that after the first winter of operation in 1961, a huge oil truck delivering the bunker fuel to the tanks under the new building crushed the pipes, and they were never used again.

Thus, the plumbing work of W. E. Emerson and the pipe laying work of Acme Construction, which was said at the time to be the "largest [pavement heating] installation of its kind in the city," proved to be an unnecessarily expensive portion of the one million-dollar building, which otherwise has served the citizens of the city well.

MACY'S IN SAINT JOHN?

 For decades, the highlight of a trip to New York was a visit to Macy's in the downtown core. Likewise, the highlight of a shopping trip to Boston was a trip deep into the basement of Filenes on Washington Street. Most Saint Johners do not know, or have forgotten, that the downtown once had a store that combined the experience of the two big American Stores, and was known as Macy's. It wasn't the grand structure of its American cousins, to be sure, but it emulated them in its operations. Whether it was an "official" outlet of either US store is questionable, but it sure was advertised as if it were. On December 14, 1950, this advertisement ran:

> *Play Santa with any one of the many lovely gifts in Macy's basement. And better still, it's so easy on your purse when you shop the Automatic Way. Automatic Thrifties are guaranteed to SAVE you MONEY. FIRST PRICES are ALWAYS LOWER TO sell goods QUICKLY, thus we avoid 3 Automatic Reductions of 25% after 30, 60 or 90 days. Leftovers are given to local charities after 120 days. 'Our Merchandise Will Surely Go, As Our First Price Is Really Low.'*

The Might City Directories of the era listed the store for the first time in 1943, at number 215 Union at the corner of Waterloo. Besides the location, it showed the owner as Jack Macy, though in subsequent years he is listed as J. I. Freeman. The name of the shop changes from time to time, too, becoming Macy's Ladies Shop at one point and Macy's Specialty Store toward the end of its existence, which was sometime in the mid-1950s. At that point, too, there is a second shop at 7 Waterloo, specializing in ladies' "ready to wear goods." Off-the-rack clothes were a novelty and a selling feature then, since it was still common for women to make or refurbish clothing for themselves and their families.

The Might City Directories show this business for the last time in 1957, at which point it became the Smart Shop, on Union Street, and the Waterloo Dress Shop around the corner.

An appeal in March 2013 for those with recollections of the Macy's operations resulted in comment from half a dozen New Brunswick women who verified the facts gleaned from the advertisements. In addition, Ann Walker recalled that "you could lay something away and pay on it till you needed it." That was, she thinks, a new idea at the time. Phyllis Gallop remembered walking from Rockwood Court to the store to get outfitted when her sister got married. "We checked everything out," she said, "on both the main floor and the lower-price basement." Lois Jones, who worked there, recalled Macy's as a beautiful store with gorgeous clothes. "I made twelve to fifteen dollars a week in wages at the time," she said. Faye Leaman recalled how she and her friends, who all worked at Simms, would go to Macy's on payday to shop. "Once," she said, "we all bought the same white short coats, and we all put them on and wore them as we walked from Macy's through King's Square and over to the Riv [Rivera Restaurant] for a Coke. The waitress greeted us with, 'Where was the sale, girls?' as we came in. Of course, we said, 'Macy's.'" Nancy Hoyt's recollections were of the shoe shop that was part of the Macy's operation. "I distinctly remember going with my older sister, who was trying on many pairs of shoes."

Doreen Hansen, who attended nearby St. Vincent's High School and worked at Macy's in the 1950s, brought the owner to life in her comments. "His name was Jack Freeman, and his wife Leah and two children had a lovely apartment upstairs over the store. My sister Helen and I used to babysit for them occasionally."

Her husband, Dave, recalled that he used to visit during those babysitting sessions, along with another two couples, for "quiet parties," as he called them. "We would have to leave [or be kicked out] by 10:45," he said, "as the Freemans were due back within a half hour." He wonders to this day if the Freemans knew what was going on, but concluded, "I'm sure they must have."

Likewise, Doreen is not sure if Mr. Freeman ever knew the nickname the teenage girls who worked there had for him. "He liked to slick his hair with Brylcream, so we called him 'Greasy,' but never to his face," she laughed.

DID YOU KNOW?

The temperature was sub-zero, but nylon fever was high on the morning of Tuesday, February 19, 1946, when hundreds of Saint John women lined up on King Street outside Manchester Robertson Allison's big department store. For the first time since the war, nylons were available in quantity. Police were on hand to "keep order," but had little to do, the newspaper report on the event noted, as the crowd was not inclined to stampede.

MYSTERY OF THE DUCK COVE
SEA CREATURE!

In the mid-winter of 1934, residents of Duck Cove, overlooking the Bay of Fundy in Saint John West, discovered an approximately five-metre (fifteen-foot) sea creature washed ashore on the beach. It was described as having "a pigs snout, three large fins, and on its head two small eyes and two 20-centimetre horns."

The flesh was red and encased in about forty centimetres of fat. The creature had been slit open, and one of the residents "hacked a steak off the beast" and had it for lunch. Declaring it to be tasty, he planned to cut off a roast for Sunday dinner, according to a report carried in the *Evening Times Globe* on February 24, 1934.

The creature was named "Old Wobby" by some of the five hundred adults and children who climbed down the steep embankment to the beach for a closer look and to carve their initials in his tough hide. One old salt said it was a "Gampus," as he had seen many off Cape Cod while at sea. However, Dr. McIntosh, curator of the New Brunswick Museum was leaning toward identification as a "Beaked Whale."

A few days later the *Globe* carried a follow-up, noting, "'Old Wobby' is different from any other known species of whale." Dr. McIntosh had to admit he was stumped and that he was appealing to experts at the British Museum. "He's a beaked whale," said Dr. McIntosh, "but what kind of beaked whale is another matter."

While the article notes the head of the monster was removed and added to the collection of the New Brunswick Museum, Dr. Don McAlpine, current head of the Department of Natural Sciences at that institution, has no record that ever happened. However, in 1999, McAlpine, with a special interest in marine

animals, stumbled across the 1934 *Times Globe* article and immediately recognized the photos as something significant.

Says McAlpine, "Dr McIntosh had it right, it certainly is a
'beaked whale,' but which of the fourteen species known to make
up this group?"

He noted that many beaked whales are poorly known and
all are very rare in New Brunswick waters. He added that, with
some careful enlargement of the photo from the *Times Globe* and
a review of the scientific literature, he had identified the whale
as the Blainville's Beaked Whale. He added that this was one of
the species' only Canadian appearances, and to this day is the
one and only New Brunswick sighting recorded.

As to why the specimen is not found in the museum's collection, he could only speculate. "Dr McIntosh was an insect person,
so perhaps found the large, greasy, putrid whale too much to
deal with." He added, "To this day I still cry into my beer knowing that the skeleton and other tissues of that whale apparently
did not find their way into the museum research collection."

DID YOU KNOW?

Cartographer Champlain wrote about another
monster when in Saint John, the story of the
Gougou, shared with him by the Aboriginal peoples.
Champlain never saw it, but he did draw monsters
fitting the description on all the maps he made of
the area.

THE TELEPHONE GIRL AND THE IRATE CUSTOMER OF YESTERYEAR

The telephone has become such a tool of modern life that we scarcely realize that it has only been just over a half century since it was necessary to engage a telephone switchboard operator to make most calls. NB Tel's prime office of operations for the province was in Saint John, and hundred of young women had their first jobs as telephone operators. The job was not an easy one, as can be seen from this excerpt from the *N.B. Telephone News* of December 1944, when E. Stevens wrote of the abuse operators took when they could not make the connections the customer wanted.

If you were a telephone girl and stood at a switchboard in a rush hour, and if someone took the telephone off the hook when there were forty other people doing the same thing within a minute, and if that person, having waited ten seconds should ask if you were asleep, how would you like it?

If you were a telephone girl and you had eighteen telephone wires, with plugs at the end inserted in eighteen connections to enable thirty-six people to talk, and there were seven of these close together and a couple of people hung up their phones and you pulled out of the maze the wrong wire and cut two people off from talking, would you think it fair if either of the victims swore a little and asked if you were out late last night?

If you were at a switchboard and someone asked for a connection and the person desired did not answer the telephone, and if the party calling rattled the receiver rapidly, instead of slowly, as he should, and the rattling of the phone hook did get into communication with you, would you like him to ask if you thought you we're enjoying a "pink tea?"

It would, no doubt, do us all good to put ourselves in the other person's place whenever we are inclined to find fault with the public service. Gas, electric light, trolley car, telephone, it is all the same. The employees generally do their work as well as they can.

A thought as relevant today as it was in 1944.

SUBURBAN STORIES

Author's note: Greater Saint John has a population of 140,000, of which 70,000 are found in the suburbs of Rothesay, Quispamsis, and Grand Bay–Westfield. Fifty years ago, most people living in these areas were summer cottagers, so there isn't yet the stock of stories that are found in the city. However, there will be, and these few will be told in generations to come.

A BRIDGE FOR GONDOLA POINT?

Just over a hundred years ago, in September 1912, the *Saint John Globe* published a map of the Kennebecasis River Valley which showed proposed routes for railway bridges to cross the Kennebecasis at either Perrys Point or Gondola Point. The merits of both were briefly laid out in fifteen column inches (thirty-eight centimetres) of type below the map. Basically, both of the routes would require a bridge for the freight from the Grand Trunk Pacific and the Canadian Southern Roads that could come via the Valley Railway. This line was to follow the St. John River from Fredericton. At some point between Oak Point and Westfield, a bridge would be built to cross the St. John River, and the rail line would then cross the Kingston Peninsula to one of the two bridges under consideration. The line would then link to the long-established Intercolonial Railway (ICR; Moncton to Saint John), which would run to the proposed Saint John Courtenay Bay Docks. None of this happened in the ensuing years and to this day, there is still only talk of a bridge at Gondola Point.

Perry Point Bridge would cost $250,000, and Gondola Point $1,000,000, due to deeper water which would require a cantilever-type bridge as piers could not be sunk. The disadvantages? Though lower in cost, the Perry Point route would add ten kilometres to the distance the trains had to pull freight in order to reach the ICR line into Saint John. Saint John businesspeople were urged to push for the Gondola Point crossing as a cost-effective way to move freight into the city.

ACADIAN CLAIMS CARVED ON ROCK

In the deep woods of Hammond River Park off the Neck Road in Quispamsis, there is a mystery waiting to be solved. Anne Hickey of Hedley Lane knows of a circuitous route though rocky cedar woodland to a moss-covered boulder some claim is an ancestral boundary marker for the area's Acadian settlers. On the rock is inscribed an eighteen- by twenty-four-inch (46 x 70 cm) rectangle, subdivided into four smaller rectangles, which some believe represent the division of the land into four sectors for four founding families. It is believed the area was an Acadian settlement, and that settlers were trying to develop a canal not far from the rock, which would have jointed the Kennebecasis and Hammond Rivers, but they left the area in the great dispersion of 1756. It is thought that most of the families that lived in the Quispamsis–Meenans Cove area went to Edmundston. However, this is mostly speculation based on oral tradition.

Brunswick Nursery owner Duncan Kelbaugh heard the story when he was working with Atlantic Association of Landscape Designers to lay out the park in the 1980s, and said they were careful not to place any pathways near the rock.

In a 2009 interview with Mrs. Hickey published in the *Telegraph Journal* on the matter, the writer, like Kelbaugh, was careful not to give an exact location so that the rock would not be defaced. As part of story, it was asked if any one could help with the interpretation of the rock's Acadian history, but the writer received no responses. Thus, it remains a mystery.

Gondola Point is named after a canoe once used
to transport people across the Kennebecasis,
where the present twin ferry system operates connecting Highway 119 in Quispamsis
with Highway 845 on the Kingston Peninsula.
According to Dr. William MacIntosh, director of
the New Brunswick Museum from the 1930s to
the 1950s, the name should actually be Gundalow,
as that was the proper name for the type of boat
early New England settlers built.

HOCKEY STAR DANNY GRANT OPENS KENNEBECASIS VALLEY RECREATION CENTRE

With all the hoopla surrounding the qplex in Quispamsis—and
every bit of it well deserved, for this is surely a great addition to
the opportunity to enjoy leisure activity in the Saint John area—
the role the venerable Kennebecasis Valley Recreational Centre
has played may be overlooked. Tucked behind the Rothesay High
School, it was the project of the town of Rothesay, in co-operation with the Villages of Renforth, East Riverside-Kinghurst,
Fairvale, and Gondola Point. At the opening of the $410,000 com-
plex on July 14, 1972, it was said to be the first such collaborative
building in New Brunswick.

The committee, headed by Richard Oland, thought big as they invited famed NHL star Danny Grant to cut the ribbon at the opening ceremonies. Grant was arguably one of New Brunswick's most famed native sons in the professional hockey world. Having grown up in Barker's Point, he entered the NHL with the Montreal Canadiens, playing part of a season in 1968, then was traded the Minnesota North Stars, where he blossomed. He won the Calder Cup as rookie of the year just three years before he came to Rothesay and went on to amass 535 points in a 14-season career. There are probably guys playing in the old-timer's leagues in the rink today who were young boys agog at Grant when he opened the complex over forty years ago.

MR. BEAVER CANADA MEETS THE MICKELBURGH BEAVERS OF BARNESVILLE

Emulating a hero of her childhood, Grey Owl, Nancy Mickelburgh set out to tame the beavers that she saw swimming about the lake near her Barnesville home. She had to be very patient, holding a slender stick with an apple on the end of a string till the beavers were enticed to try it, then shortening the stick each night until the beavers came ashore for their treat. After about four years of slow progress, she had what seemed a family of four who would come to her for snacks and even do tricks. Some of them, with names like Marilyn, Big Daddy, and Anne Murray, would even let visitors feed them, and in time there were plenty of visitors who came to the remote lake to see the spectacle.

Two children are able to approach the wild beavers at Grove Hill when they come for supper.

Thus, it seemed only proper when the founder of Beavers Canada, Gord Hannah of Winnipeg, came to visit Saint John to talk about the implementation of the Beavers program in New Brunswick, that he should be taken to meet Mr. and Mrs. Mickelburgh's pet beavers.

On an October afternoon in 1974, Abe Goss, myself, and my son Derek took Gord Hannah to Grove Hill where the beavers went at five o'clock for feeding. It was our hope that Gord would meet the creatures the movement was named after.

Gord was not disappointed, though he was a bit shy at first until he saw four-year-old Derek feed Big Daddy. That gave him the courage to hop over the fence and do the same. As he wrote later, "I followed him [Derek] and offered the carrot stick to Big

Daddy. Big Daddy set up on his hind legs with his tail for support and reached out his hands to the carrot. He began too munch... the carrot was a tender morsel. He was so careful. His hands had full control but I let the carrot go before he got to me."

Then Gord tried a second carrot, and at that point, he was more confident and noted, "It was a wonderful thrill to feel Big Daddy's trusting hands on mine. It was like shaking hands with another person. Beavers Canada had met the beavers at Beaver Lake Refuge!"

The same thrill that Gord experienced was exactly what thousands of others had when they came to the site, but, unfortunately, it is not an experience that is possible today. When the Mickelburghs died, the beavers soon went back to their natural ways of feeding, and today, if you visit the site, you'd never know it was once the refuge of beavers or the place where the Beavers Canada founder met the real thing.

Scouts Canada has 18,000 Beavers enrolled in this beginner's level of the scouting program across Canada.

PAVING THE WESTFIELD ROAD

We take paved roads for granted today, but as recently as four generations back our forebears travelled on soggy wheel-swallowing mud in spring, and axel-breaking, dusty, and rutted gravel roads in summer. This was the case even between major cities, like Saint John and Fredericton, so it was big news in 1934 when it was announced that the river road leading from Saint John to Westfield would be paved. At that time, this stretch was prime cottage county, and most of the summer sun seekers reached their bucolic riverside retreats by train, which still did almost hourly passenger runs between Fairville Station and Welsford. However, as the years passed, more and more were getting second-hand Model T's or A's as it was far more convenient than the sometimes kilometre or more walk from the various stations like Acamac, Martinon, or Pandemac, especially when carrying groceries or tired children.

A *Telegraph Journal* article of August 31, 1934, shows an asphalt plant, set up by the Dufferin Paving Company at Acamac, about midpoint along the paving project. That location was chosen as the liquid asphalt could be brought to the site by railcar. The rock was already there, but had to be quarried and crushed from nearby hills. Sand had to be added, then everything was mixed and heated to 500 degrees in a blast furnace till it was ready to be conveyed in 5.5-ton lots by truck which, the article said, were driven "hurriedly to the point where it was to be laid."

Now you have to imagine how noisy all this rail car shunting, quarrying of rock, mixing of rock and sand, the conveyor belts to move it to the furnace, and the blast of the furnace itself must have been for the cottagers, as the *Telegraph Journal* article does not mention the noise. However, the photo that accompanied the article clearly shows another nuisance of the plant: huge billows of very black smoke being emitted from the stacks of the operation. That was the price paid by the residents of Acamac for the delight of driving the first paved roads in their area. On some portions of the road, it isn't hard to imagine that the 1934 pavement is still being driven over to this day.

One of the more famous summer residents in the Acamac–Belmont area was Donald Sutherland. The cottage his family summered in, and where he wrote and acted in his first plays, still stands almost unchanged on the shore of the St. John River, and can be rented from its current owner by those who would like to sleep where Sutherland slept.

SHE SANK TO THE
BOTTOM OF THE SEA

The last verse of an eighteenth-century English sea shanty, brought to these shores by the sailors who worked on wooden ships, was about mermaids and their ability to send vessels down to Davy Jones's Locker. It sings as follows:

> *"Then three time round went our gallant ship, then three times round went she,*
> *And the third time she went around, she went to the bottom of the sea!"*

Though the song was written two hundred years earlier, it still applied to the shipping scene in Saint John as recently as the 1980s.

In was in 1982 that the thirty-nine-metre-long *King Fisher II* was tipped to its port side and stuck in the mud not far from the venerable covered bridge that crossed the Milkish Creek at the southwest end of the Kingston Peninsula. For seven years the residents of the area had complained of the unsightly appearance of the vessel which its owner, Maurice Fisher of Rothesay, had intended to use as a riverboat on the St. John and Kennebecasis Rivers.

The *King Fisher*, a fairmile, was built in 1944 and featured a hull of double three-quarter-inch mahogany planks. It was designed to be used as a coastal patrol ship on the St. Lawrence, and originally had light armaments and small depth charges on board. The boat did not sink during this first life. Its second life was as a tour boat during Expo '67.

Where the ship worked from the end of Expo until the mid-1970s is unknown, but the boat's third life began when it came to the Saint John area with the hopes that the riverboat era, which had ended in 1945, could be revived. Suitable docking facilities could not be secured for such a lengthy vessel, so the *King Fisher* was anchored in the Milkish, and subsequently sold to a new owner, which would have given the boat a fourth life. It never happened, and he never came to retrieve the vessel, which eventually sunk in the shallows of the creek. (That was not the deep blue sea the song speaks about, but a temporary sinking.)

After long agitation by local residents, the government hired Alpha Diving and Salvage to dispose of the vessel in March of 1982. They originally planned to drag the vessel across the ice and burn it in a quarry, but that didn't work. They had to wait until high water in May to begin the process of righting the vessel, plugging the holes in the hull, and floating it down the river, through the Reversing Falls, and down to Lorneville, where it was sunk and became part of a breakwater to protect the lobster boats using the Point Road Wharf.

Thus, after "three times round" the *King Fisher* "went to the bottom of the sea!"

The vessel is still very much a part of the lore of the Kingston Peninsula, and bits of the ship are still to be found from its days in the Milkish Creek. While it lay in the channel, pieces of the very nice mahogany with which it was constructed were stripped off and ended up in the homes of skilled woodworkers on the peninsula. These pieces have been worked into furniture and decorative pieces enjoyed to this day.

SUBURBAN MORNA AND KETEPEC, ONCE SHUNNED AS HAUNTED

In 1933, writer U. V. Caulfield related a story of a tragedy in the Morna–Ketepec area that led to the belief the tracks running through the woodland adjacent to the highway were haunted. In his story, Caulfield relates how the first railway cars arrived for the North American Railroad at a specially built terminal at Westfield beach, and how, afterward, the railway developed that beach as a pleasure beach. That is a well-known fact to this day, and even now there are those living who can recall the last of the Sunday School picnics held on the grounds. The area was especially favoured by west Saint John churches that came from Fairville station to Westfield Beach by rail coach until the 1940s.

Caulfield's story was not about that beach, but about an incident that occurred in the hills cut out between Ketepec and Morna in order to reach that beach. The line, of course, had to be as level as possible, so the hills had to go. It was "man killing work" Caulfield wrote, adding, "hard liquor flowed over many bars to hard men, men who counted brawn, not brain, the greater asset." It was on that section of the line, he noted, that a cluster of cabins known as "The Shanty Down Grade" developed, and where an army of men toiled for years.

These men were "railway builders [who] encountered the herculean task of drilling by hand, and blasting with powder a succession of hills composed entirely of solid rock, of which is now a succession of rock cuts."

It was in this shanty town area there "occurred a most gruesome tragedy, the details of which are best left untold." Too bad, for it would be good to have such details!

The result of the tragedy was that for years after it took place, "the spot where it occurred was supposed to be haunted."

This haunting was, Caulfield said, a "discomfort and inconvenience to the succeeding generations young men, whose 'courting days' happened to take them from Grand Bay to Sutton," now known as Ketepec.

He explained that taking the track though the cut would shorten the distance considerably, yet noted it was more to the liking of the young men of the time to take a "tortuous and round about road to get by the haunted cut rather than take any chances with the terrible apparition that was supposed to inhabit it at night." However, the story concludes with the tale of one man who did take "a chance on the direct route and arrived at the cut about 11 p.m."

The gent was surprised to find the cut much darker than he imagined it would be, but had no brushes with any phantom until almost through. That was when, as Caulfield wrote, "the darkness was rent by such a clattering and clashing he thought the whole side of the cut was opening up to swallow him."

The gent reported that "I took my hat off, and it would have been a darn smart ghost that could have reached Grand Bay when I did."

The next day, as was the custom of railway men, the cut was routinely examined for obstacles on the rail, for it was normal just after it was opened for rocks to slip down from the hills. As Caulfield put it, "Patrick [Paddy] Lynch—a section man—who by the way was living in the last of the shanty town cabins, while patrolling the track, found a large bunch of rocks, which, loosened by the frost, had clattered down the side of the high cut and spewed out on the track."

As logical a reason as you might want to hear to explain the noise the walker had noted...but not one the courting men of the area were wont to believe. For hearing his tale of how the still and dark night was rent by the "clattering and clashing" and of how he managed to barely outrun the phantom to the safety of his Grand Bay home would only serve to amplify their belief in the haunted cut at Ketepec–Morna.

THE MUSICAL BUCKLEY FAMILY

Quispamsis couple Bob and Murial Buckley brought a musical family into the world in the sixty years they have been together, and their children have brought much pleasure not only into their lives, but into the lives of music lovers all over New Brunswick— in fact, all over the world.

When they began playing publicly in the 1960s, the Buckley Family consisted of Tim (bass), Kathy (cello, piano), Chris (violin, viola), Peter and Joanne (violin), and John and Ellen (cello). At one point, family members made up a substantial part of the New Brunswick Youth Orchestra's string section. Chris and Joanne were founding members of the Saint John String Quartet, and Chris is still a member today. In fact he makes his full-time living as a member of that quartet and principal violinist with Symphony New Brunswick, of which John and Ellen are also members. Though Chris is the only full-time musician these days, the others, in addition to holding full-time jobs in teaching, financial planning, and the IT field, have, over the past four decades, performed with musical groups in Canada, the United States, Europe, and Asia.

The Buckley Family at the 2012 Christmas Times Concert at St. Alphonse in Hampton. Credit: Richard Graves.

Many who know of the family's musical prowess and their value to the musical life of the community believe the annual Christmas Time Strings program at St. Alphonse Church in Hampton is their crowning achievement. They have performed the concert during the week following Christmas for twenty-two years.

It seemed natural, then, to ask Father Kevin Barry, the pastor there, to give his comments about this event. He recalled that the Buckley's were "enthusiastic supporters" when he was at St. Mark's in Quispamsis, and "like a few other families, they followed me to St. Alphonse when I was posted here in the early 90s."

He added,

> However, I don't recall how the idea developed for a musical concert, but I guess it would have been a natural thing for a family so gifted in music. They were part of the music at worship, and I suppose it came out of that. Still," he said, "it's more than a musical show...they bring such sense of wholesomeness to the presentation...they make the audience so comfortable with their back and forth banter as one or another introduces the pieces they will play. As soon as we announce the date in early December, people put it on their calendars. They come from all over the south of the province. It has become a seasonal favourite with people...the church is always full, even if we have a bad weather night. And everyone gets a lift...it's like a tonic in a season that is sometimes just so hectic."

Reg and Jean McKenzie have only missed one of these concerts in the past two decades. "I think it snowed too hard one time," Reg laughed, when asked about the annual event, "and we could not travel out from Quispamsis. We hated to miss it," he added.

The McKenzie and Buckley children got to know one another when their mothers, Jean and Muriel, served on a committee for school improvements in the area. "They had a real gift for music from a very early age," Reg said, "and along with that, they really liked sharing that gift. I think that's how the Christmas concert began, it just wasn't enough for them to do it at home... the joy they had in performing just had to be shared. It's infectious, and for us, it marks the season better than any other event we attend."

Commenting on the Christmas concert, John, who played professionally in Ontario but is now working in the world of finance in Saint John, said, "For us, it's a delightful time, too. It is the only time we play together as a family nowadays. It's nice now that we have another generation at the concerts, as Kathy's children, Monica and Natalie, are playing with us. We hope we will be able to do it for years to come."

Nowadays, the Buckley musical gifts are heard in Alberta, too where Joanne lives and freelances with the Red Deer Symphony. Tim, who lives in Calgary, has two children who are receiving recognitions as singer-songwriters in the country music genre.

Thus, it would seem certain that the musical Buckley family will continue to delight audiences both in New Brunswick and further afield for years to come.

TWO ENDINGS FOR FAMED KENNEBECASIS SCULLING RACE

 The four burly Saint John fishermen were laughed at when they entered a sculling race in Paris in 1867, but smirks turned to surprised looks when they easily won that race. In consequence, they were thereafter known as the Paris Crew. The men, Robert Fulton, Elijah Ross, Samuel Hutton, and George Price, went on to win many more competitions, but were topped in Lachine, Quebec, in September of 1870, by a crew from Newcastle-on -Tyne, England. They immediately scheduled

a rematch on the smoother waters of the Kennebecasis on August 23, 1871. There was heavy betting on the outcome, but no one was sure what it might be. Poet Byron DeWolf was not taking any chances...he prepared two endings for his rhymes describing the event, so no matter which way it went, he could sell his work immediately as a broadside. This is how he ended the poem in case the Newcastle crew, headed by James Renforth, won:

> *Hurrah, the oarsmen are in sight, crowds shout and cheer and run.*
> *Again the famous men of Tyne the victory have won;*
> *The white silk pocket handkerchiefs again in triumph wave*
> *But still New Brunswick honoureth her twice defeated brave.*

But, as it turned out, James Renforth suffered a heart attack tying to catch the Saint Johners, and DeWolf's second ending it the one that was used. It read:

> *Hurrah, the oarsman are in sight, crowds shout and cheer and run.*
> *And all along we hear the cry, "the Bluenosers have won";*
> *Let's all take Harding by the hand and wish him many joys.*
> *In weal and woe he is the one to back the Bluenose boys.*

WHENCE CAME THE ROCKWOOD PARK BEARS?

A zoological garden was one of most popular attractions soon after Rockwood Park was established in 1894. However, the zoo fell on hard times, as did the entire park. First came the First World War, then the Depression, and then the Second World War. While the attractions in the park were badly run down from years of neglect, the very strong and ornamental bear cage, built early in the nineteenth century, still stood in the fifties and needed bears to delight visitors. That's when Walter Armstrong and Snooks Caulfield came to the rescue, according to a story shared by Armstong's widow, Rosalind, when she was approaching her centennial year. In her own words, this is the tale she told on March 31, 2010.

We shared a camp on Little John Lake with Snooks and Eloise Caulfield. One of the adventures Walter had out there was on one occasion when he and Snooks went out to open up the camp for spring and summer and they came across three cub bears that had been abandoned by their mother along the way. They brought two home, and they put one of them up in a packsack and tied it up in a tree at the camp. One of the cubs that was in Walter's trunk had nearly chewed through into the front of the car by the time he got to home here in Westfield. They secured them and they went back and got the other one. We had all three of them here, Walter made a sort of cage in the woodshed and we tried to feed them milk out of a baby's milk bottle, but they would have none of that. So anyway, they had really sharp claws, so we put them in cages and I put one can on the end of stick and passed it down and they fought to get into that one, so I put three cans on the sticks in the end so they could each put their heads in, and then one would seem to say to the other, 'you've got something better than I've got,' and they'd fight over it. We had school kids here, they brought them from the school each day, up from Westfield school, a class each day. The bears were quite an attraction.

Now, at that time there was a bounty on bears for $10.00 apiece, and they got their bounty on the bears, but then they didn't kill them. They were too cute, so eventually they sold them to the zoo in Rockwood Park.

As Rosalind had shared a story with me, I thought I should share one with her, so I told her that those bears probably ended up in Moncton. About 1953, the province suggested Saint John close the zoo and open a campsite as they predicted the New England rubber-tire traffic with campers and trailers would be the next wave of tourism. And they were right. The Horticultural Association donated the bears to the Magnetic Hill Zoo in Moncton, and they were among the first animals of what is arguably the best zoo in the province today.

It was deer shipped by ferry from Saint John to Grand Manan Island that established the deer population in that Fundy isle on May 10, 1933.

SUBURBAN GOVERNMENT HUMOUR

In the nineteenth century, residents often did roadwork as a way of paying their tax bills, but when there were no more taxes to be worked off, the government would offer contracts for the work. In this instance, the work was on the road from Saint John to Fredericton at Blagdon just where the Kings County line met the Queens County line. It is considered at suburb of Saint John today, barley twenty minutes from the city centre, though in 1873, when the poem which follows was penned, it would have been a half day's stagecoach ride. This government official had a bit of flair in calling for the work as you will see. His call read:

On Thursday, the 26th of June,
At 11 o'clock in the forenoon.
On the Nerepis Road I will attend,
Having a few dollars thereon to expend
The lowest bidder the job will get,
The work by auction will be let,
Commencing if the day be fine,
At Blagdon, near the Queen's County line.

SAYINGS IN AND AROUND SAINT JOHN

"YOU'RE HAVING A DOLLAR NINETY-NINE MOMENT."

Lawyer Glen Larsen operated the Piskahegan Kayak Company out of St. George, and his principal clients were Saint John women seeking outdoor adventure in and around the many islands in Passamaquoddy Bay. They could relate to his Stedman's five-and-dime store description of a dollar and ninety-nine-cent moment, which was the terminology he used when they were overcome by the scenery of the bay or were enjoying his famous lobster or clams cooked in seaweed while on one of the remote beaches of the area.

"HAYWIRE SQUARE"

This is a derogatory name for Haymarket Square, originally a two-acre rectangular patch of greenery with pathways around and through it. It was originally where farmers sold hay to city dwellers with horses, thus the "hay market," which became, over time, Haymarket. It was gussied up by a civic-minded group called the Polymorphians to mark the city's centennial in 1883. Though bisected by a spur line of the Canadian National Railway, it remained a pastoral experience until the roads around it were converted to New Brunswick's first roundabout in the early 1960s as part of urban renewal. The redesign, likely the result of urban renewal chief Don Buck's English background, was such a puzzle to motorists it was given the sobriquet Haywire Square. It was again redesigned in the 1970s as an entranceway to the Throughway, and for all intents and purposes, no park-like amenities remain to be enjoyed, and the name Haywire Square has all but disappeared.

"PURELLO, PURELLO."

The call used by teenage hostesses in the 1940s at the Reversing Falls Trading post to alert staff, but not the public, that their boss, Mr. Wilson, was crossing the Reversing Falls bridge and would soon be in to check on them. "That meant we found something to do even if there was nothing to do," Gwen Farnham said in an October 2004 interview, recalling the pleasant days she spent working at the location. Purello was one of the extracts the H. W. Wilson Company bottled at their uptown Saint John factory.

"SKE'PING THE GONG"

The unauthorized ringing of the fire bell, which, before the Great Fire of 1877, was located at the head of King Street. When done properly it was rung in patterns to alert the volunteer firefighters where the fire was to be fought. However, its open location led to many false alarms. Though a watchman was hired to prevent the unauthorized ringing of the bell, it just made the task a bit of a challenge, and when it was done, it would be said that the boys had "ske'ped the gong" once more without reason. "Skelp" comes from the dialect of north England where it means a "sharp, quick blow."

"THAT WILL BE A FOGGY FRIDAY."

Not a very appropriate saying in Saint John, which is Canada's third most foggy city, for it means that you will not get the thing you desire until its foggy and Friday...which could be often.

DID YOU KNOW?

Two sayings my dad used may not be known outside the family, but they were regularly used when
I was a lad. Dad would say "I have a bone in my leg"
when he wouldn't come out in the yard to play sock
ball with my siblings and I. Of course, we took it he
had something wrong, not knowing everyone has
bones in their legs. The other one was "You'll get
that when my ship comes in," used to indicate we
would not be getting something we wanted until
he could afford it. As our home overlooked the harbour, we thought Dad owned one of the ships that
we'd see making their way past Partridge Island
and into the west-side piers.

"GOIN' OVER TOWN"

This is the west sider's term for uptown Saint John's King Street
shopping district, as in "I'm goin' over town to MRA's to see
Santa in Toyland."

"MET ME AT DUKE AND DOCK."

Directions given when you didn't want to meet someone at all, as Duke and Dock, while a nice piece of alliteration, don't ever meet. In fact, Dock Street no longer exists, as it was renamed St. Patrick Street to honour Saint John's Irish settlers.

"HUBBA HUBBA DING DING, MEET ME AT THE HEAD OF KING."

Unlike the Duke and Dock, this one worked when it was invented as a jingle to promote by King Square Jewelers on Charlotte Street opposite King's Square, and thus near the head of King. The store is gone, but the head and foot of King are still valid descriptions used in the city as meeting points.

"UPTOWN SAINT JOHN"

This is every Saint Johner's term for the city core, or what most people call their downtown. Said to be used for the King Street Shopping District as it is a steep hill—the "shortest, widest, steepest Main Street in Canada," according to tourism literature. The other explanation given is that in times past, when this was the chief shopping zone, you could not get there from any place in the city without going "up" a hill.

Uptown Saint John. To the left are modern skyscraper-type buildings and to the right, the city that was built after the Great Fire of 1877, which remains much as it was constructed between 1877 and 1882.

The portion of the uptown at right of the above photo is known as the Trinity Royal Preservation District, and has been designated as having the best intact collection of Victorian structures in the country by Heritage Canada.

"SAY SCHWARTZ AND BE SURE."

Every singer who appeared on the CHSJ Radio and later CHSJ TV's *Uncle Bill and his Junior Radio Stars* was given a bottle of Schwartz peanut butter, as the jingle of the product was sung. The Halifax company no longer produces what was arguably the best known, and, some would say, the best-tasting peanut butter of all time in Saint John and through the Maritimes.

"THE GREATEST LITTLE CITY IN THE EAST"

Mayor Elsie Wayne's creation during the ten years she served as mayor of Saint John to promote the city she was certainly proud to lead. She used it everywhere, especially during the years when Saint John placed first in the National Participation competition in the 1980s, and in the 1990s when she was one of only two elected Conservatives in the whole country.

The present mayor, Mel Norton, uses a similar boastful term, referring to Saint John as the "Renaissance City."

"THE LOYALIST CITY"

This term is often used to describe Saint John in a historical context, as the city was founded in 1783 by those who fled America after the American Revolution. In the early 1950s, a publicity campaign, aimed primarily at the road traffic that travelled from the Eastern US, saw dozens of six-metre-tall Loyalist men standing beside the highways leading into the city to promote attractions like the Reversing Falls, the New Brunswick Museum, Rockwood Park, and Martello Tower. These are still the city's prime attractions but, due to pressure from other founding or building groups, only one tall-as-Paul Bunyan Loyalist man remains today at the Reversing Falls.

"SAINT JOHN: CANADA'S MOST IRISH CITY"

One of the groups who did not like the prominence of the English symbolism of the Loyalist Man were of course their long time foes, the Irish. This motto reflects the influx of some forty thousand Irish who passed through the city following the famine in 1847. Each March, their descendants proudly proclaim their heritage in one of the country's most frenzied St. Patrick's Week celebrations.

"THERE'S A LOT OF BARBER ON THE WATER."

This saying is in reference to sea smoke, or sea mist, which forms as vapour on the water in the Saint John Harbour in very cold conditions. It is not an expression that is heard today. Even back in 1940, when Ian Sclanders noted it in the Man on the Street column he conducted in the *Evening Times Globe*, he had to consult Dr. William McIntosh of the New Brunswick Museum to find its meaning. McIntosh said it was in reference to the sea smoke resembling the shaving cream old-time barbers used to whip up on the faces of customers in the days of wooden ships, when it was common for men to have shaving done in the barbershops, not at home.

In winter, when there is mist on the water, there is often sunlight, too: Saint John is the sunniest city in Canada during the winter months.

"SIMMS CORNER COLLEGIATE"

A reference to the cluster of ornate Victorian buildings, originally called the Provincial Lunatic Asylum, later the Provincial Hospital, which dominated the hilltop overlooking the Reversing

Falls at Simms Corner. They served as Canada's longest-standing institution for mental illness from 1848 until they were replaced by a new facility in South Bay in 1998.

The Simms Brush and Broom Company ceased operations at the plant which gave the corner its name in November 2013.

"DOWN ON THE TRAFALGAR STEPS"

The Trafalgar Steps was a stairway that led to the ferry to Saint John West from Market Slip. They received the designation after the English victory at Battle of Waterloo on October 21, 1806. Though there is no ferry service at the site, steps still exist leading to a floating dock at Market Slip, and a plague on the stairway identifies this as the location of the original Trafalgar Steps.

"SAINT JOHN—CANADA'S AIR-CONDITIONED CITY"

A positive spin on the often cool and foggy weather that persists some years during the summer months, and also, the benefit of

The Trafalgar Steps still lead to Saint John Harbour at Market Slip two hundred years after the event they celebrated occurred.

being adjacent the cool waters of the Bay of Fundy which seldom exceed 7°C in summer. Average daytime summer temperature in Saint John is 22°C and it drops to 11°C at night, while inland in Fredericton it is 25°C in the daytime, and drops to 14°C at night, thus the claim of natural air conditioning.

"MINISTER'S FACE"

The nickname given to the craggy face-like appearance of the east side of Long Island found in the Kennebecasis River opposite the town of Rothesay. It rises steeply almost seventy-six metres out of the river. Why it seemed to people like a man of the cloth rather than a lawyer, doctor, or Aboriginal chief is unknown, but the name is well engrained in local river lore. It has remained an area attraction since it was first pictured in tourism promotions in 1909.

"TEED'S SQUIRREL CAGE"

The derisive name given to a traffic roundabout. The route forced 32,000 cars a day travelling west in the early 1960s on North End's Main Street to make a one-kilometre detour in their quest to get to Saint John (west) via Douglas Avenue and the Reversing Falls Bridge. The plan simply backed cars up and did not make the passage any quicker, so it was likened to running in place on a wheel like a caged squirrel. Eric Teed was the mayor at the time. He was a man full of ideas, and though there is no proof the roundabout was one of them, it nonetheless got his name due to his leadership position.

"DON'T GET CAUGHT IN THE TIDE STREAK."

Advice given to anyone going out skating on the lower stretches of the St. John or Kennebecasis Rivers where, after the river freezes, the rising Bay of Fundy tide pushes the river water upstream, and it seeps up over the ice a metre or so off the shorelines and creates a yellowish, water-filled channel. While the biggest danger is getting your feet wet if you skate through the tide streak, they are still best to be avoided lest the skater's weight breaks the weakened ice under the water.

"THE ICE IS WETTING UP."

Another term heard along the shore is "wetting up," which is when the weather warms after the ice freezes in the fall, and the river water then flows up and over the newly formed ice, wetting it down. In the spring, as the ice softens and melts, the same thing happens as the weakened grayish ice begins to sink and the currents open a channel in the river.

"DID YOU HEAR THAT BURST?"

Riverside residents will also talk about a "Burst" which happens when it gets extremely cold and the ice suddenly shifts, creating a huge roar that can be heard kilometres away. Observation will show that a shore-to-shore crack has developed. In typical circumstances, one portion of the ice will be higher than another. "Bursts" can be extremely dangerous to snowmobilers and have resulted in some serious accidents over the decades.

"THE COLD WATER ARMY"

The Cold Water Army was a nickname given to child-age members of the Sons of Temperance Association in the 1840s in both Fredericton and Saint John. A write-up in the *Reporter* newspaper in March 1847 about Fredericton noted, "an interesting sight was presented on our streets on Saturday afternoon—the children belonging to the Cold Water Army, numbering about one thousand, marched in processions to hear a lecture by Mr. Gough." A few months later in Saint John, the *Reporter* noted the "Cold Water Standard had been raised" and there are "now upwards of one hundred and fifty names enrolled," clearly showing the Temperance movement was making gains even in the hard-drinking port town of Saint John.

Almost 23 percent of tax filers in Saint John made a charitable donation to one or more social or religious agencies in 2010.

"THEM'S FERRY BOAT SAILORS"

Jack Sweet recalled this moniker as a derogative nickname for the captain and crew of the ferry *Loyalist* that crossed Saint John Harbour during the Second World War. These men had been excused from war service due to the importance of the link across the harbour. Those who used the nickname thought it easier service than those who were called overseas.

Ferries crossed Saint John Harbour continuously from 1789 until the ferry *Loyalist* ceased operation on December 31, 1953.

"TAKE THE QUEEN'S SQUARE LOOP AT THE DOG CART."

After travelling from the city centre by ferry, the link for buses to Beaconsfield, Fairville, and Milford was via a streetcar driven by Jim Ready, nicknamed the Queen's Square Loop. It began its run at the ferry floats at the head of Rodney Slip, near the "Dog Cart" where longshoreman could buy hot dogs, sandwiches, and coffee. It then ran along Union, West on Rodney, South on Ludlow, West on Tower, South on Lancaster, and through Queen Square—thus its name. The name was still used until the 1950s, though, during a strike in 1921, the tracks through Queen Square were torn up and not replaced. Bus service replaced the streetcars in 1948, but the name of the route didn't change until the bus service was cancelled when the ferry stopped crossing the harbour at the end in 1953.

BY THE NUMBERS

Saint John currently has a fleet of 53 buses whose 63 drivers provide 102,000 hours of service annually, carrying 3 million passengers to their destinations.

"BE QUIET OR YOU'LL WAKE THE DEAD IN CARLETON."

Donna Lee Bury's mom used to quiet her down with this warning when she was a youngster growing up in Saint John. She has no idea where it came from. There were three graveyards in Carleton, the portion of Saint John West east of City Line to the harbour, but in Donna's youth, only one was visible: the Old Carleton Graveyard. Although the first mayor, Gabriel G. Ludlow, is buried there, in her youth it was a sadly neglected site and hardly a place she or her mother would visit. Nonetheless, the warning was given often.

"THE STORE WITH THE MAGIC EYE, THE WELCOME DOOR, AND THE INVISIBLE DOORMAN"

These were advertising descriptions used when Carl A. Robbins opened what he called the "Maritimes' newest and Greatest Drug Store" at 17 Charlotte Street in December 1940. It had the first electric eye-operated door east of Montreal. Routine in the Maritimes today, it was a novel feature then. Combined with an eclectic mix of merchandise, air-conditioned premises, and a better than average lunch counter, it made Robbins the store of choice for uptown Saint John shoppers needing pharmaceutical goods, patent medicines, beauty products, or the latest toy craze to put under the tree.

FIRSTS, FACTS, AND FOIBLES

TECHNOLOGICAL LAYOFFS NOTHING NEW IN SAINT JOHN

We hear of layoffs today due to computer technology replacing workers, but workers have been displaced by new methods for a long time. The 1851 Saint John census noted that several of the trades and occupations reported in the 1840 census had passed into disuse. It named the manufacture of soap, candles, boots, and shoes, and the tanning of hides as industries that had ceased operations. The report concluded that the workers had been "largely replaced by machinery."

THE SAINT JOHN 100,000 CLUB

We hear about men and women going west these days for work. This is not a new trend in Saint John. Just over a century ago, the city of Saint John held a "Back to New Brunswick" week from June 9–14, 1912, the idea being to attract those who had left the city to return home. The *Seattle Post Intelligencer* conveyed the story to those living on the American West Coast that the city had formed a 100,000 Club and was determined to get those who had left the town back and build the population up to the 100,000 mark. A *Post* editor, a former New Brunswicker, wrote, "After resting on the rocks doing nothing but watching the Bay of Fundy tide rise and fall for 100 years or more, the old city has awakened." The horse races, baseball games, and aquatic sports that followed during "Back to New Brunswick" week may have been fun, but did not result in a spurt of growth to the 100,000 mark.

DID YOU KNOW?

Mayor Elsie Wayne was a great Saint John booster, and the *Authorized Biography of Elsie Wayne* by Linda Hersey had the highest number of book sales at a launch of any book in Canada in 1998. Neptune publisher Henry Flood brought the book out, and he says the sales figure of 476 books in two hours is a record for a Canadian book.

WHAT'S THE CONNECTION BETWEEN SAINT JOHN'S HARBOUR STATION AND TORONTO'S ROGERS CENTRE?

It is the forty-three-centimetre wide plastic chairs in both locations, and though many Saint Johners have sat in them in both locations, few know this fact. The chairs in both facilities were manufactured by the same company in Berwick, Maine.

In 1880, Bill Phillips of Saint John was the first Canadian to play in the major leagues and the first to hit a home run. Since then almost 250 Canadians have been in the "show."

SAINT JOHN'S MOST OVERLOOKED PIECE OF ARTWORK

In the grassy but always cold and shadowy lot west of Loyalist House at 120 Union Street is a huge metallic depiction of the Loyalist flag that is surely the most overlooked sculpture in Saint John. It was a fifty-five-thousand-dollar gift to the city from Parks Canada and officially dedicated on May 18, 1983, the city's two hundredth birthday. Seldom is there is anyone seen looking at the work and taking the time to read the plaques that tell the

Loyalist story. Perhaps now that Peel Plaza is opened across the street, the sculpture will get more attention from those passing by on Union Street.

THE MARKET SQUARE TIMEPIECE

In contrast to the Union Street artwork, John Hooper's seven-metre creation at the entrance to Market Square is without doubt the city's most visited artwork. In all seasons of the year, people sit and pass time among the statuary, which is exactly what Hooper hoped they would do. Unless told the secret by those in the know, few figure out that the way to tell time is to look to the very top ring, and note where the serpent's head and tail are joined.

SAINT JOHNER'S POETIC LINES GRACE ENTRANCE TO PARLIAMENT BUILDINGS

Two lines from a four-stanza composition by Saint John native John Almon Ritchie, KC, are carved into the main portals of the Parliament Building in Ottawa. Ritchie had no idea that architect John Pearson had chosen his work until Lieutenant Governor MacLaren asked where the lines had come from. When told of the source, it was a great surprise to MacLaren to learn a fellow New Brunswicker had penned them. At the time of his discovery, the job was still in progress and the lines were supposed to be covered up by a board. But someone removed it, and for all to see are the words "The wholesome sea is at her gates, Her gates, both east and west."

Only two political figures have public images in the City of Saint John. A statue of Father of Confederation and local MP Sir Samuel Leonard Tilley stands in King's Square, and the carved face of Mayor Sylvester Earle looks across to the former City Hall from the third floor of the Chubb Building on the corner of Prince William and Princess Streets.

The city's first female mayor was Elsie Wayne, elected in 1983. She served ten years as chief magistrate, and this makes her the longest-serving mayor the city has had since being incorporated by Royal Charter in 1785. She later became a long-time Member of Parliament for the city.

The longest-serving councillor on the present Common Council is also female, Shirley McAlary. First elected at a councilor in 1992, she was immediately appointed as deputy mayor, became mayor in 1993, and served in that role until 2004 when she was defeated by Norm MacFarlane. She returned to council in 2012, and is still serving as a councillor at large giving her, to the beginning of 2015, fifteen years of service.

The Bell family has the longest service to the city as Members of Parliament. Tom Bell served in that role from 1925–1935, and his grandson, Thomas Miller Bell, served even longer, from 1953–1974. Murray MacLaren is second, with fourteen years served, and Elsie Wayne third, with eleven.

Though only forty-two years old, Portland–Simonds Progressive Conservative MLA Trevor Holder is the longest-serving provincial politician in the Saint John area. Holder was first elected in

1999, and he has served the north end and Millidgeville area of the city since. He has been on both sides of the government and until recently he served as minister of Tourism and Parks.

RADIATOR-SITTING COMPETITION WHEN SAINT JOHN HIGH OPENED

When the $650,000 Saint John High School opened on Prince William Street in September 1932, one of the concerns of the teaching staff was student behaviour. As a summary of one set of minutes notes, "everyone knew how to behave in the Union Street building, but the huge new school posed a whole new set of problems." One they likely never foresaw was a student fundraiser that was reported in the February 15, 1932 *Evening Times Globe*'s popular Man on the Street column, which quoted a story in the school's paper, *The Red and Green*. The item read, "A new endurance record was set when Charles Cook, of Mr. Denham's room, won a radiator-sitting contest. He sat on a hot radiator for one minute and forty-five seconds. Joe Clark won a close second in this sizzling-hot race."

HOW BLINDMAN LAKE GOT ITS NAME

 In the depression of the amphitheatre-type hillside on the Loch Lomond Road just before Lakewood Heights is a four-hectare lake. In the 1840s when John Garey brought his family from Ireland to escape the potato famine, they settled on the land behind the nameless lake. Though the family never held the title to the property, they cleared the land and developed fields overlooking the water as farmland. Farming not being enough to support a growing family, John also worked as a stonemason in Saint John. Pat Garey, John's great, great, great grandson, relates that John was blinded as a result of a job site accident. Sometime after that, the lake took its name from John's condition, and became known as Blindman Lake.

SUCCESSOR OF NEW BRUNSWICK'S EARLIEST HOSPITAL STILL SERVING CITIZEN'S HEALTH CONCERNS

In the south end of Saint John at the corner of Wentworth and Britain Streets stands the venerable Turnbull Home, which serves as a long-term care or nursing home for fifty residents. While it has a modern wing, the original building dates to 1882 and was built to replace the Kent Marine Hospital, established in 1822 as New Brunswick's first hospital. As the name indicates, it served seafarers. The cost of operation was paid by a levy on all shipping coming into the province of one cent per ton, but it wasn't enough to meet the upkeep. The hospital was in sad shape by the Great Fire of 1877, but to the chagrin of many, it was one of two buildings to survive that conflagration. However, just after the fire, real estate baron William Wallace Turnbull donated what was considered the largest charitable donation in the city's history for a new building to replace the tired 1822 structure. The original building was razed, and the fine brick-faced Seafarer's Hospital was built on the site. By 1899, no longer needed for seamen, the hospital became known as a "The Saint John Home for Incurables." It has since served in varied capacities as a senior's home for those in need of long-term care.

KING'S SQUARE'S POPULAR AND UNIQUE BENCHES

 For decades the benches that lined the perimeter and walkways of King's Square were unique to the City of Saint John. They were made in the city's works garage as a winter keep-busy project when employees were not plowing or sanding streets. The benches were painted annually during the cold season, using a colour known as "city green," as everything the city was responsible for—fences, public stairs, litter barrels—were all a standard shutter green. In the 1980s, the benches were painted in all the colours of the rainbow and were delivered to the Square on a specially constructed wagon that was only used twice a year—when the benches came out in spring and when they were put away in the fall. It was known as a "Settee Wagon," and like the benches themselves, was a creation of the inventive minds of the Rothesay Avenue Works Department.

That the benches were popular is clear from a report in the *Evening Times Globe* noted on March 20, 1940. "Hardly had the big benches been lifted out the specially horse drawn "settee" wagon... and been placed about the Square when the first occupants appeared on the scene—shoppers, mother's airing their babies, retired business men, schoolboys, transients—and within a few moments the place looked just like as though summer had been only yesterday." Two days later, the paper reported on a Sunday storm that left twenty-five centimetres of snow on the newly placed benches!

NEW BRUNSWICK'S LARGEST BOY SCOUT TROOP

Officially, a troop of Boy Scouts could not exceed four patrols of eight boys, but in the 1950s when the war babies reached Scout age, there simply were not enough sponsors to handle all the boys who wanted to get into the movement. Thus, group committees turned a blind eye to numbers. So long as leaders were available, troops operated outside the regulations. However, no troop did so as grandly as the Centenary Queen Square United Church in the heart of uptown Saint John. With the whole of the South End and East End to draw from, (then with a population of about thirty thousand) the Troop expanded and expanded until it had fifty boys in December 1950, and was listed as the largest in the province.

FIRST MARRIAGE IN SAINT JOHN COMMEMORATED BY GRAVESTONE FAR FROM CITY

A gravestone in the very remote Gosline Cemetery at Smith's Creek, north of Sussex, is an unlikely place to find a story about the city of Saint John. But there it is, carved onto marble stone by Saint John's preeminent stonecarver of the early nineteenth century, J. Milligan. The stone tells the story of the first marriage in the City of Saint John, which occurred on April 4, 1784. Genealogists do not think the stone is the original one, but likely placed later, some years after the death of the couple, by the

This stone has details of Saint John's first marriage and is found in the Gosline Cemetery near Sussex.

family of Andrew Stockton and his wife, Hannah. They also question if the couple are actually buried there. However, no one doubts the story the stone tells. This is how it reads:

Leut. Andrew
Hunter Stockton
Who was born in Princeton,
New Jersey, Jan 3rd
Ad 1760, and died at
Sussex Vale, May 8th 1822
Also Hannah
His wife born in
The State of New York
& died in Kings County
October 14 A.D. 1793
Aged 25 years & 1 mo.
Luet Stockton was married in
The City of St. John then called
Parrtown on the 4th of April 1784 by
The Honourable George Leonard which
Was the first marriage that ever
took place in that city.

In 1883, J. W. Lawrence published a commemorative book on the history of the province under the title *Footprints.* In it he noted that the Stocktons had fourteen grandchildren, forty-three great-grandchildren, and fifty-four great-great-grandchildren then living in New Brunswick. Imagine what those numbers would be now after another century and a quarter has passed!

DID YOU EVER PLAY "UNDER THE SHEETS?"

No, this entry will not make this into a banned book, though the name of this game played on the Kingston Peninsula surely sounds a bit risqué. It was, however, a way for locals to have some fun with come-from-aways who summered at Holderville, Long Reach, near the Cedars, or any of the many other cottage enclaves in this suburban Saint John location. Recalled by Frances Carvell, the game involved two participants laying on the floor and being covered by a sheet. One was from away, the other a local who was in on the trick. The come-from-away would be told he would be tapped with a paddle, and upon sitting up, would have to try to determine who had done the tapping. He would assume it to be one of the watchers but all along it was the person under the sheet with him doing to task. "The locals," Frances recalled, "had a great laugh as the stranger guessed this one and that, but never the person under the sheet with them."

FIRST TALKIE IN SAINT JOHN... IT WASN'T AT THE IMPERIAL AS IS OFTEN SAID!

The first 100 percent talking movie to be shown in Saint John was *The Donovan Affair*, staring Jack Holt and Dorothy Revier. It debuted at the Queen Square Theatre on Charlotte Street on April 29, 1929.

This comedy/murder mystery started as an Owen David stage play before being adapted for film. The *Evening Times Globe* described it as having "sheer entertainment, a lot of thrills, laughter, and any amount of excitement," with "suburb acting," and "voices well pitched and intelligible at all times." The show advertisement noted it was a "Hear and See" film, a "100% Talking picture," and featured "12 famous stars." The cost of admission was 25 cents for the 2:30 matinee and 35 cents for the evening shows which played at 7:15 and 8:50 for three days. The film had only been released April 11, and at the time, many theatres were not prepared to make an investment in new equipment for talkies. However, they soon acquiesced, as talkies became the rage, some films making profits of 5000 percent over costs.

FOG CITY

Loyalist Day, which marks the founding of Saint John on May 18, 1783, might have been a week earlier on May 11, which is when the ship *Two Sisters* arrived off Partridge Island in the outer channel to Saint John Harbour. But due to a stretch of the city's infamous fog, most of the settlers could not disembark until the 18th. That's when Sarah Frost wrote in her diary, "We began to see the fog come on, for that is natural to this place."

Indeed the city is Canada's third-foggiest, with only St. John's and Halifax being slightly foggier. In July of Canada's Centennial Year, there were 506 foggy hours of a potential of 744. Most Julys have 175 hours of fog, and even that is enough to create sombre citizens, who, when the fog lifts a bit, say things like "It might be bright," or "Hooray for the Sunshine," instead of "Hello" as a greeting to one another.

PHOENIX THEATRE WELL NAMED

The Phoenix Theatre on Exmouth Street operates a lively dinner theatre program in the former 1857 Methodist Church, which was a survivor of the Great Fire of 1877. In fact, it was the only Methodist church in the core of the city to open for services after that fire on June 20 burned down 1,400 buildings in proximity to its east end location. It survived a second fire in 1964, but not the dwindling membership, which dropped from 321 families in 1961 to 125 in June of 1978, when it closed for good. Of course, the phoenix is the famed bird that rose from the ashes, and that is why it can be said that the current theatre is aptly named.

NEW BRUNSWICK RED HATTERS FOUNDED BY GRAND BAY GIRL

Pat Perrin is the founder of the popular Red Hat organization in New Brunswick. In February of 2003 she saw an article about Sue Ellen Cooper, who founded the Red Hat Society in California in 1997. Cooper, who was known at the time as the Exalted Queen Mother of the Red Hat Society, gave Pat permission to form the Bay West Chapter in Grand Bay, and to call herself its "Queen." Since then, hundreds of ladies have become members of the society, whose only aim is for ladies over fifty to get together and enjoy one another's company. As Pat said in an interview in May 28, 2004, "We put on our red hats, purple dresses, and we smile away our troubles."

EARLY MUSICAL LIFE IN SAINT JOHN

We take singing in church today for granted, but when Wesleyan Methodist musician Stephen Humbert moved with the Loyalists from New Jersey to New Brunswick in 1783, churches rarely had singing. Musical historian Edward Erb, speaking in Saint John at an Early Music concert in 1977, said, "At that time, about the only instruments the Loyalists would have brought with them were fiddles, jews harps, perhaps a virginal, and the occasional wind instrument." He suggested that none of these were used in church settings. What might have been used, though, Erb said, was singing from the Bible's book of Psalms, and it would take a skilled leader with a good ear to do that. Certainly it seems Humbert would have excelled at leading such singing.

There is no certainty that he led the church music but it's likely, due to his other activities. By 1796, he opened the Sacred Vocal Music School in the city and in 1801, he compiled for publication a book of hymns suitable for the church, titled *Union Harmony*. It was the first Canadian music book with English text. It is also possible he might have, from time to time, been a guest of Ward Chipman, who held soireés at this home atop Chipman Hill during which the latest songs from London would be performed.

In any case, Humbert was indeed a pioneer in the musical field in Saint John, and the tradition of choral singing is still strong in the city to this day.

JAMES QUINTON—FIRST CHILD OF ENGLISH PARENTS TO BE BORN IN SAINT JOHN

 On the night of August 26, 1762, Hugh and Elizabeth Quinton arrived with a party of twenty-one New England settlers in what was to become Saint John. That night, the first child of English parents was born at Fort Frederick, approximately where the west entrance to the Harbour Bridge is today. The child was named James, who went on to become a well-respected carpenter and was elected to serve on Common Council and as a Member of the Legislative Committee.

The property Hugh Quinton received was huge and stretched across the west peninsula from the Bay of Fundy on the south, to South Bay on the St. John River to the north. When the Loyalists arrived, Hugh had cleared fifteen acres on Taylor's Island, today known as the Irving Nature Park. About 1815, Jessie Quinton, the youngest son of Hugh and Elizabeth, built the fine, spacious, rural Georgian home near the hilltop, where it still stands, at number 1260 Manawagonish Road.

The property served several generations of Quintons and was a productive dairy farm for years. However, as the city spread westward, farms were swallowed up by suburban development and the last of the Quinton property became Quinton Heights, one of the best locations to live in Saint John when it was developed in the late 1940s.

BATTLE OF QUINTON'S CORNFIELD

A long told tale of Saint John West is the so-called Battle of Quinton's Cornfield. It is so engrained in the local lore of the area that on August 22, 1961, the *Evening Times Globe* published an editorial stating that Saint Johners were guilty of not giving due recognition to some stirring chapters of the area's history. This chastisement was in response to a letter from A. Carle Smith that described a 1778 raid by Americans who had landed at Musquash then marched to the Quinton land in Saint John West, supposedly to seize the area for the US. However, Gilfred Studholme and a force of the Loyal Highland Regiment, who were hidden in the cornfield and routed the enemy, thwarted this plan. Smith suggested a memorial stone commemorating this incident be placed in Quinton Heights. The *Evening Times Globe* pointed out that the following year would be the two hundredth anniversary of the arrival of Simonds, Hazen, and White, the founders of Saint John, and that there would be benefits to residents and tourists alike if incidents like the Battle of Quinton's Cornfield and the other raids during the Revolutionary War were publicized.

A plaque was indeed placed in the public park in Quinton Heights, but it only commemorated the settlement by the Quintons. It made no mention of the Battle of Quinton Cornfield, because, despite it being a well-known story, no authentic documentation exists to prove it actually occurred.

EDWARD ROWE SNOW'S BIG WALK

Edward Rowe Snow (1902–1982) of Boston was America's pre-eminent collector of sea stories involving pirate treasure, ghastly ghosts, and terrible shipwrecks along the Atlantic Coast of North America. His search for stories brought him to Atlantic Canada on numerous occasions and to Saint John more than once. His most memorable visit to the city was in 1949, when he came to make a thorough examination of the famed Reversing Falls, which are now more aptly called the Reversing Falls Rapids. Prior to that trip, he'd visited his doctor and been told he was 40 pounds overweight at 231 pounds. In his book *Strange Tales from Nova Scotia to Cape Hatteras* he tells how he started out from Saint John's Admiral Beatty Hotel and walked to Portland Point, where he examined Fort La Tour. He then walked along Straight Shore to the Reversing Falls where he climbed down the rocks to river level to better appreciate the phenomena. The walk continued to Martello Tower, then he left the city and was in Pennfield by evening. So began the first day of his walk. The *Evening Times Globe* of August 2, 1949, reported he was back in Boston after walking 1,327 kilometres in 23 days. His weight had dropped 2 pounds a day as he averaged 58 kilometres per day.

Snow's account of the walk in his book, dated September 7, 1949, says he travelled for 38 days, walked 1,863 kilometres, and averaged 64 kilometres per day, losing 42 pounds in all. It is clear from the map he attached that he did walk beyond Boston to Cape Cod and toward Block Island, as, upon reaching Boston, he was determined to keep off the weight he had lost.

Of the walk, he wrote that besides "gaining the trim figure which was mine a quarter century ago," one of the benefits was the opportunity "to get acquainted with people I would have otherwise missed altogether." On the downside, he wrote, he was offered thirty-eight rides, but turned them down and "was nearly run down by eleven different automobiles." Overall, he noted, "It was an experience I shall never forget."

A SAINT JOHNER INVENTED THE PROCESS OF FREEZING FISH

Most reference sources say that Clarence Birdeye was the man who gave us frozen fish, however, a Saint John man, Enoch Piper, was freezing and sending salmon to the New York market in the 1850s, thirty years before Birdeye was even born. Piper developed a freezing process and built a plant in the Valley area of Saint John, not far from the old Victoria Rink and adjacent to the 1853 European and North American Railway terminus. He brought in salmon from the northern New Brunswick rivers to ship out to the American market. The Boston firm of Brown and Seavey tried unsuccessfully to have Piper build them a plant in the Massachusetts capital, but he refused, even though he was offered eighty thousand dollars to do so. So they simply built it themselves using his idea. He sued. The court case went on for six years but was decided by the American courts in favour of the American company. It cost Piper forty thousand dollars to fight the case. Over time, the Saint John firm lost its grip on the US market, and Piper ceased to operate. However, firms in Halls Harbour, Nova Scotia; and Newcastle, Bay du Vin, and Bathurst, New Brunswick that he'd been working with continued to follow his process, which involved using ice and salt. Some accounts of the process of freezing fish do give credit to Enoch Piper as one of several who had discovered it before Birdeye perfected it about 1925.

DID YOU KNOW?

Two Saint John men were responsible for the introduction of the well-known sanitary product, Dustbane. While now based in Montreal, the company had it origins and first factory in Saint John, starting in 1908. Chester E. Pickering and George W. Green combined a readily available waste product from Saint John sawmills, sawdust, with chemicals to create a green, pine-scented sweeping compound that quickly became a staple in factories, schools, and to some degree homes, as a cleaning agent.

FIRST REGISTERED AUTO IN NEW BRUNSWICK

On May 9, 1905, J. Walter Holley of 116 Coburg Street in Saint John was the first to register a motor vehicle in the province of New Brunswick, one of only twelve vehicles registered that first year it was required. His vehicle was 1905 Rambler, which several antique auto books describe as a sizeable twin-cylinder machine with front bonnet, one of 1,500 built that year. He imported it from Thomas B. Jeffery's factory in Kenosha, Wisconsin, which had been building bicycles until the motorcar came along. What Holley paid for it is not known, but in the US at the time, the vehicles sold for about $800. His registration fee was $5, which is the equivalent of $175 in today's money.

That same motor vehicle registration noted Regina Holley as a chauffeur, which simply meant a driver, and thus she became the first woman in the province to be licensed to drive a vehicle.

FIRSTS & FACTS

ABRAHAM GESNER—GAS LIGHTING AND THE ELECTRICAL FUTURE IN SAINT JOHN

In May of 1840, famed geologist and discoverer of kerosene Abram Gesner made a proposal to light the city of Saint John with gas. Alderman Porter took the very long report to council for consideration, and council, even back then, took the route they so often take: it ordered, after a few brief observations, that the report "stand over for further consideration before discussing its merits." The discussion took several years, it would seem, for the first street lighting did not occur until September 18, 1845, when several lamps were lit on King and Prince William Streets.

In the meantime, the forward-thinking Gesner was busy considering the future, the age of electricity that his great mind and experimentation allowed him to foresee. In December of the same year he approached council, he gave a lecture at the Saint John Mechanics' Institute and did several demonstrations of the potential of electric power. The *New Brunswick Courier* covered the demonstrations and describes only one: the effect of rubbing a rod on a silk handkerchief and then placing the rod near a magnetic needle, making the needle revolve rapidly without being connected to any electrical apparatus. "The facts communicated in this lecture should be known to every person in society," the *Courier* noted in closing.

Saint John Energy has quietly provided Christmas
lighting to the citizens of the city since the first
Christmas tree was lit in King's Square in 1924. This
was the first public tree to be lit in the province. At
the same time, lights were placed on trees in the
lobby of the General Hospital on Waterloo Street.
Eventually a tree was placed on the dome of that
structure and was a Christmas highlight for decades.

WILDCATS STILL IN SUBURBS OF SAINT JOHN IN THE LATE 1940S

It seems hard to believe today, but wildcats were still preva-
lent in the Coldbrook area of Rothesay Avenue in east Saint
John as recently as the late 1940s. No area of the city has
changed as much as Rothesay Avenue in the past six decades. First there was Parkway Mall in the early 1970s, followed by McAllister Place in the late 1970s, and finally, East
Point Shopping Centre with all the box stores that surround
it. No self-respecting wildcat would take a chance with the
traffic these stores generate today, but in February 1948, the
Telegraph Journal reported that there were so many of them in
the area that hunters were "digging out old traps," in order
to claim the bounty of ten dollars per animal caught, and an
additional fourteen dollars for the pelt.

A real effort was on to clear the district of the animals, and it intensified when a report was made that one of the beasts had "entered into the kitchen of a house near Coldbrook Post Office where the door was ajar, walked around a cradle in which a baby slept, and walked right out again." The mother of the child thought it was stray dog in her kitchen until she went to the post office and saw a wildcat carcass on display there. She was left wondering, the paper noted, "how her baby escaped the attention of the wandering cat." In another incident, a wildcat wandered onto the highway and sat down in the track of an oncoming bus. The animal stared down the bus but moved when it came close. Even then, the cat only moved a bit up the road before sitting again. This sitting and staring process was repeated four times before the cat went into the woods. Forest rangers believed the combination of a deep snow base and the good number of pheasants in the area was what attracted the cats just five kilometres from the city centre.

HOW SAINT JOHN PROVIDED DEER FOR GRAND MANAN

Before settlers came, Grand Manan Island, out in the Bay of Fundy at least a dozen kilometres from the mainland (it's nearer Maine than New Brunswick), was not home to most of the animals that cavort on the mainland. Over time that situation has changed and most mainland animals have been introduced for trapping or hunting. That includes deer, but the first ones brought to the island in the 1840s were so overhunted that they all but disappeared. They were reintroduced in 1909 but were still struggling, so over the years other attempts were made to beef up the island's deer population. One such occasion was in the mid-1930s.

The Rockwood Park Horticultural Society, whose Zoological Garden was home to a herd, decided it was too expensive to continue to feed the deer after losing their city grant. At first they were going to slaughter them (along with a black bear), but someone came up with the idea of transferring the deer to Grand Manan. The attempt to round them up did not go well. A newspaper report noted, "'Billy' the big buck, went off on his own leaving his doe to mourn him." Billy jumped an eight-foot fence when the staff came to round up the two bucks and three does they wanted to ship away. Eventually, however, the deer were successfully crated in huge wooden boxes, loaded aboard the Grand Manan ferry at the East Saint John dock, and shipped off. Although the newspaper commented that the deer were probably seasick on the voyage, they finished the story on a positive note, saying that the deer would be released in heavy woods between Seal Cove and Grand Harbour. Once in the woodlands they flourished and are still providing good hunting to this day.

NOT THE GOOD OLD DAYS

So began a small column in the *Saint John Daily Star* of September 18, 1903. What followed was a tongue-in-cheek description of a dance that had been held in the Globe Hall in the South End of Saint John the previous evening, which they labelled a "most surprising affair," as "no one was more than half killed, very few were drunk, and none were carried home." The Globe Hall dances were notorious affairs and always received attention from police. The *Star* noted that the officers on duty the previous night had "scarcely recovered from the shock of not being called in to stop trouble."

The article concluded that the dance ended at 1:30 a.m., a "very reasonable hour for Sheffield Street," and to the surprise of all, the crowd dispersed very quietly. In summary, the *Star* had a "strong suspicion some reformer has been at work in Lower Cove," perhaps thinking a religious revival among the people of the area was the reason for the change in conduct at the dances.

PONY EXPRESS IN SAINT JOHN?

Yes, Saint John was the terminus for a pony express–type of operation in the year 1849. That's when Saint John had a telegraphic connection with Boston, but Halifax did not. So, when the latest in British news (correspondence and newspapers) arrived by ship in Halifax, it was taken to Digby by relays of horses. The information would arrive on the south of Fundy shore in about eight hours. The mode of transport would then change to boat, and the material would travel north over the Fundy by ferry to Saint John, where the details could be telegraphed to Boston. This procedure meant the information in the papers arrived in Boston about thirty-five hours faster than leaving the materials on ship sailing from Halifax to Boston. However, when Halifax got telegraph service, the pony express faded into oblivion.

For 127 years, there was no longer a pony express operation, however, in 1976, a historic reenactment was conducted with the co-operation of the Joseph Howe Festival in Halifax and Loyalist Days Festival in Saint John. Saint John Mayor Edis Flewelling greeted John Pelham of Halifax, who represented the pony express carriers who, many years before, brought the mail to Saint John. In this instance, Pelham brought greetings from communities and personalities from all across Nova Scotia to Saint John. As this historic ride was never repeated, it can be said that Pelham was the last pony express rider to visit the Saint John area.

The first use of an x-ray in Saint John occurred at the General Public Hospital on Waterloo Street on June 28, 1902. It was a Roentgen ray apparatus. There were many skeptics about the new technology, so to convince them, Dr. Will Ellis used his own hand to demonstrate the process, now a staple of medical treatment.

HOW SAINT JOHN WAS PEOPLED IN EARLY TIMES

The first census done in what is now Nova Scotia and New Brunswick, which included the Saint John area, was conducted in 1671. Then known as New France, it showed that there were 392 men, women, and children living along the coast of Acadia, and no white men at all up the St. John River. The next census was conducted 15 years later, in 1686, and numbers had more than doubled to almost 1,000, of which half were in Port Royal. By then, the La Tours were long gone from the fort at the mouth of the St. John, and Sieur de Martignon, his wife, Jean, and his 24-year-old daughter, Marianne, lived there. Jean was a daughter of La Tour, but not the offspring of his relationship with Marie Jacqueline, who had died at the fort in 1645. Just three years after the 1686 census, Fort La Tour was again abandoned as Martignon had died and his family moved away. When the Acadian expulsion occurred in 1755, there were only a few Acadian families in what was to become Saint John, and they fled up river to join perhaps 200 people living inland. By 1758, when Colonel Robert Monckton came to claim the territory for England, he reported there were none in the area to oppose him. Simonds, Hazen, and White, English-speaking American settlers from Massachusetts, arrived in 1763, and the area was once again populated. However, just how many came with them is uncertain.

BY THE NUMBERS

While as many as 15,000 Loyalists came to
New Brunswick in 1783, various records indicate the population of Saint John was only
about 5,000 during the war of 1812. It was up
to 20,000 by 1840, and 38,000 by 1861. Had
the population continued to double every
twenty years, Saint John would have a population of 5 million today.

LAST CATTLE DRIVE IN
SAINT JOHN WEST

Ngarie Nelson shared the story of the last cattle drive in Saint
John west which was told to her by her husband, Dick. He recalled
it happening in 1946 when he was only five years old. At that
time his father, Ivan Nelson, and his family moved from a farm
near Lancaster Avenue to South Bay. The cattle were pastured
where the Lancaster Mall stands today. The route of the drive
was as follows:

- Up to Simms Corner
- West on Main Street past Church Avenue
- Continue west along Manawagonish Road, passing under
  the maples (then only saplings)

- At Kierstead's Corner, sometimes called Manchester Corner or Purdy's Corner, turn north and go out to Manchester Avenue and over the Canadian Pacific tracks at Bogg's Crossing
- Continue past the golf course at Ridgewood
- Just before the Baker Castle, head uphill over a dirt road and cross the CP rail line a second time
- Arrive at destination, the hill overlooking the marshes of South Bay.

Today, there is no sign that the farm ever existed, nor are cattle driven from farm to farm over the streets of the city.

LOCAL PRODUCTS DINNER

The Fundy Fisherman of November 15, 1929, carried a report of a dinner tendered by New Brunswick Publishing that featured a completely local menu in an effort to impress noted editor John M. Ermic, visiting from Western Canada. Surprisingly, most of the products could still be on a banquet table to this day. The fare included:

- Connors clam chowder
- Rankine's biscuits
- Sardines on toast
- Slipp and Flewelling boiled ham
- New Brunswick potatoes
- New Brunswick squash

- McCready mixed pickles
- Perfect prepared mustard
- Griddle cakes with Crosby's molasses
- Pacific Dairies ice cream
- Red Rose coffee
- King Cole tea
- Gurd's ginger ale
- Corona chocolates

All this food was washed down with sparkling Sussex Ginger Ale. To celebrate the completion of this book, perhaps you might like to try a similar meal and see how close you can come to replicating the 1929 repast.

DO YOU RECALL?

Dominion Stores was for many years the leading chain grocer in Maritime Canada, and where many of the products noted above could be bought. It began its foray into the eastern provinces with two stores in Saint John that both opened on July 3, 1930, one on King Street and the other at Charlotte Street at Duke Street. At the time they opened, they had five hundred stores across Canada, but today they are found only in Newfoundland.

A FIRST IN RADIO FOR
SAINT JOHNERS

Travelling to Fredericton is an easy one-hour trip by highway, but in the winter that hour can be a challenge. It was even more so on the night of January 25, 1939, when the new Bishop for the Diocese of Fredericton was to be installed. As he had served in Saint John as rector of St. Paul's Church, many Saint Johners, anxious to go but unable to make a winter trip, were delighted that they could witness the ceremony by simply tuning into the CBC station (CHSJ then). That occasion was the first broadcast of an enthronement of a Bishop made in all of Canada. The Bishop was the Rt. Reverend W. H. Moorehead, who served until 1956.

A photo of the occasion that appeared in the following day's *Telegraph Journal* shows there were some Saint Johners who did travel to the ceremony, including Reverend Harold H. Hoyt of East Saint John, Reverend Canon J. V. Young of Mission Church on Paradise Row in Central Saint John, Reverend F. J. LeRoy of Fairville, which would be Saint John West today, and Reverend Craig Nichols, whose specific location is not given.

A STEER AND A SALOON

During the riverboat era, farmers along the St. John and Kennebecasis Rivers would not only ship produce to the Saint John Market, but put cattle, pigs, and horses aboard the boats for delivery from the Indiantown wharves where the trip ended to the merchants across the city. The cattle would be marched through the streets to their final destination at one butcher's shop or another. Most went without incident, but on a delivery on August 8, 1901, a curious steer went amuck. As he marched up Main Street, he caught an odour coming from Ed McBeath's saloon that enticed him to break ranks with the other creatures and go off to investigate. Stopping outside the saloon, he had a good sniff, liked what he smelt, and charged inside to get closer to the source of the odour.

What happened inside is not reported in the news column that brought this incident to life, but when the steer came back onto the street, the report noted, "that intelligent animal emerged looking much more comfortable and happy like. He licked his expanse of jaw in a satisfied manner and wisely winking one big peaceful brown eye at the assembled crowd, went on the rest of his last journey very quietly."

It would seem, reading between the lines, that the patrons quickly vacating the premises might have spilled a few beers on the floor. Though this reporter seems to have taken some poetic license with his account of the steer's emergence from the saloon, one cannot doubt the facts that the steer did do something unusual.

A SAINT JOHNER WAS THE MAN BEHIND THE BRYLCREEM JINGLE "A LITTLE DAB'LL DO YOU"

In 1961, George Burditt, like most men of the era, had a couple of tubes of Brylcreem in his bathroom cabinet. His wife, noticing them, reminded him that the company was having a contest, and was looking for a jingle to promote their hair product.

George got busy and wrote a little rhyme and sent it in. It read.

> Brylcreem, a little dab will do you
> Simply use a little on the hair.
> The girls will all pursue you
> You may have to court them by the pair.

What happened next is best explained in his own words.

> Two days later they phoned me and said I'd won a bright red MG sports car. The day after that, I met a guy who wanted to buy such a car, but only if it was red. So, I told him mine was red all right! He bought it. He lived in St. Stephen and the money I got was the down payment on my first house which was on Squires Street in Fredericton. It was a $12,000, house and by selling the car, I had $2,500 down and that looked pretty good.

In 1856, John Howe Jr. was appointed Saint John postmaster and received a penny paid by the recipient for each letter delivered, with the usual number being twelve.

FIRST AIR MAIL SERVICE IN SAINT JOHN WAS FASTER THAN TODAY FOR SURE!

On December 10, 1929, the *Evening Times Globe* reported, "Soaring into the air at 1:09 p.m. this afternoon, an airplane piloted by W. H. Irvine, a New Brunswick man, inaugurated the air mail service between Saint John and Moncton." The report noted the plane carried between six thousand and nine thousand letters on its first trip, which was an experiment being closely watched by officials from the local post office. It was said that this service would give Saint John businessmen an additional half day to answer queries from the North Shore, as the train that usually took the mail left for Moncton at 7 a.m. but the plane would leave five hours later, and mail could still reach Moncton in time to be forward and received by North Shore addresses the same day.

HOME OF THE FOUR-LEAF
CLOVER CHAMPION

Even if we have Irish blood in our veins, most
of us are lucky to see one four-leaf clover in
a lifetime. But on July 5, 1933, Mrs. Margaret
LeLacheur Robin began to pick four-leaf
clovers on her front lawn, and had a box full
of them by the end of the week. Intrigued
editors from the *Evening Times Globe* counted
186 four-leaved clovers and agreed with her
that she was the champion clipper of clovers.
She claimed they were easy to find everywhere...she'd picked two hundred from Mount
St. Helena in Washington state and found
them easily right across North America.
Though considered lucky by most people, Mrs.
Robin told the *Times Globe* she "was not sure
whether the clovers brought her good luck, or
whether her good luck brought the finding of
the four leaf clovers." In any event; she sure
found many more than most of us do.

GARGOYLES IN SAINT JOHN?

There are only two true gargoyles in Saint John, although there are many ornamental decorations on the buildings in Trinity Royal that look like gargoyles and are worth gawking at, and many guides make the mistake of calling all such figures gargoyles. However, the majority of these are grotesques, though some are depictions of the building's owner, such as the image of George Chubb on his building at the corner of Princess and Prince William. True gargoyles must drain the roof water collected in the eaves and spout it out of their mouths, away from the building. Gargoyles are usually fanciful human or animal faces. In Saint John, these are found only on the former home of the famed Rankine biscuit family at 210–212 Germain Street.

DID YOU KNOW?

The 1951 viaduct that provided an overhead passage over the busy rail tracks that led to Union Station was torn down to make way for a more modern overpass in 1971. George Chittick was hired to dispose of the concrete, and mayor of the day Stephen Weyman convinced Chittick to dump the concrete at the Royal Kennebecasis Yacht Club where it formed the base of a new wharf still in use to this day.

GAS VS. ELECTRICITY

Though Saint John did not have a power plant until 1884, the idea of electricity in the was already a topic of discussion in 1878, when the *Saint John Globe* carried a poem that pointed out the advantages of electric power. We just take light and power for granted these days, but this points out clearly what our ancestors had to deal with. It read:

From noxious vapours, odors vile, and imminent explosion;
From under heaps and smuts and smoke and sulphurous corrosion;
From bleared eyes and bleached cheeks and sickness melancholic;
From belching fires and naked forms and carbon diabolic;
From hiseous gasometers and poisonous suffication;
We welcome thee, to set us free,
Electric Innovation.

LADIES DID NOT TAKE THE MILFORD FERRY AT INDIANTOWN AT SUPPERTIME!

Ferry service from Saint John West to the city proper was the only means of transport until W. Kilby Reynolds's suspension bridge successfully spanned the Reversing Falls in 1853. Still, for a largely pedestrian population, ferries remained a vital link until 1954.

A lesser-known ferry, from Milford to the foot of Main Street in North End Saint John, operated from the early 1800s until about 1936. When there were limestone mills and quarrying operations in Milford–Randolph, the ferry made sense. In 1892, when the 15-metre *E. Ross* was put into service on the 304-metre crossing, 1,000 people crossed on the first day. No doubt this was due to the novelty of a new vessel and not a daily occurrence. However, as the Milford–Randolph limestone and lumbering operations closed, the service at Indiantown ceased. Like all ferries of the era, the *E. Ross* had separate accommodation for ladies and gents on board. Marilyn Upton recalled her mother saying, "The trip at 5:00 and 5:30 was considered strictly for the mill workers, and though there was no restriction placed on women, no 'lady' would consider crossing the ferry at that time of day, as it was how they told the 'ladies' from the 'women' in Milford."

UNIVERSAL DRIVER'S LICENCE EXAMINATIONS...A GOOD GOVERNMENT MOVE IN 1961

Up until January 1, 1961, driver's licence examinations were not universal in New Brunswick, but up to each community to administer. This, of course, led to irregularities, as some examiners might be complacent while others could be much too stringent. In an official statement, the government said sixteen examiners had been trained at the RCMP's J Division in Fredericton, and would be on duty across the province. The new procedure was the result of an alarming increase in traffic accidents, particularly traffic fatalities. In 1960, there were 167 highway deaths. There were 138,469 vehicles on the road that year, thus a death rate of 11.99 for each 10,000 vehicles. In 2008, the last year for which statistics are available, the accidental deaths had dropped to 71, with 580,119 vehicles on the road; the death rate dropped to 01.22 deaths per 10,000.

In Saint John the examiners were Rupert Murdock and Harold Mayes, both Lancaster City men who did their testing out of the Provincial Building on Charlotte Street in Saint John. Many a nervous driver failed the test before leaving the grounds of the Motor Vehicle office, as driving through the narrow, L-shaped gap between the building and a retaining wall at the northeast corner of the building was a challenge. Scars on the walls and the brickwork show it was hit more than a few times.

Of course, safer cars and better highways have helped lower the fatality number, too, but it seems certain that the move to province-wide universal examinations was a positive one.

Corporal Axade Frigault, blinded war veteran from Dalhousie, New Brunswick, was chosen to open the first Veteran-operated canteen in the Saint John Post Office in March 1948. Frigault was trained at a joint program operated by Dominion Government and Canadian National Institute for the Blind in Toronto.

MEMORY OF *MANES P.* GROUNDING FADING...BUT NOT GONE!

The weather in February 1970 was as wild as it gets in Saint John, and it surprised the captain of the *Manes P.* as he tried to maneuver the 5,600-ton Greek vessel from behind Partridge Island into the safe channel of Saint John west. His crew of 30 men was surprised when they found themselves driven into the breakwater at Negro Point, with the ship listing 30 degrees to port as the waves pounded the vessel and then crashing violently into the sandy shore. At first, the men stayed on board as it was thought the vessel could be easily towed back to sea when it had settled and the high tide was in. However, in the interim, the raging sea rocked the vessel, and the huge limestone boulders of the Partridge Island breakwater punched an almost metre-wide hole in the hull. The vessel was doomed. Thousands of Saint Johners showed up to witness its final days. It did not seem to be badly broken up, but no amount of effort could budge it from the beach, and it was eventually taken apart bit by bit and sold for scrap. The captain and crew went back to Greece by air a few days later. Thousands of photos were taken of the tragedy, and they show up in collections from around the area.

NIVEN MILLER AND SAINT JOHN

 One of the memorable tributes Mrs. Francis Emerson made in remembrance of her husband, Senator Clarence V. Emerson, was a series of radio programs with CFBC and television programs with CHSJ, beginning in the summer of 1970, featuring Scottish baritone Niven Miller. The television program spread far beyond Saint John; in fact it was eventually taped in colour in Ontario and shown across North America. The radio program was heard across the Pacific Ocean in China, where it was allowed to be played beyond the so-called Bamboo Curtain, and resulted in Mrs. Emerson receiving the Asia Peace Award in New York in 1972.

Mr. Miller continued to sing and teach in his native Scotland, but has not been in Canada for many years. However, he can still be heard by those with turntables, for six of the records he made as part of the tribute to Senator Emerson are still found in the Saint John Regional Library.

ODE TO DULSE

 Cruise ship tourists are always given the chance to try dulse when taken through the city market...few will try, and few who do, like it. When the guides take a few strands of the salty seaweed and swallow them down, some of their guests almost gag. Dulse is certainly an acquired taste, and thus visitors don't really appreciate the feeling politician and lawyer D. King Hazen, QC, had for this Fundy delight when he wrote:

Ribbon like with silken sheen,
Thou floatest fair on Fundy's tide,
Pinioned to Pisarinco's rocks,
Clinging close to Quaco's side.

At Grand Manan and Pocologan,
Midst whose leaves the mermaids play,
Close- bosomed friend of the periwinkle,
To thee I sing a wayward lay.

Spray flies high and breakers roar,
Strong lean breezes stir my pulse,
On silver wings the seas birds soar,
When I smell a bag of dulse.

REVERSING FALLS UG WUG!

If the image of the Ug Wug were still at the Reversing Falls Restaurant, would you eat there?

One of the earliest stories from Saint John is about the Ug Wug that dwells in a cave deep under the Reversing Falls.

Aboriginal peoples shared the story for long before Champlain came to the area in 1604. In their tale, the Ug Wug was one explanation for the reversible rapids, and why they seldom travelled through the falls, instead developing a portage that ran behind the present Museum and down Bentley Street on the peninsula where Douglas Avenue is now.

The Ug Wug at the Reversing Falls is an enduring legend; this is the only known drawing of it. Credit: Harold Wright.

Details of the Ug Wug's appearance vary, but it is usually described as a cross between a salmon and a seal, and about thirty metres in length. In some stories, the Ug Wug comes out of its cavern only once a year, on the full moon of April when the creature feeds on the schools of gasperaux then making their way upriver to spawn.

In 1949, a huge landslide occurred at the west bank of the Reversing Falls where the city had been building a road to bypass Simms Corner, and some residents blamed the land-slide on the Ug Wug. It was said the gravel dumped in the area to build the road had filled the mouth of the Ug Wug's cave, and wanting out for a frolic, it came out...and the embankment came down.

The next year, a painting of the Ug Wug was done by artist Isabel McGuire on the walls of the Trading Post, which served as a tourism information centre for Saint John. But the painting proved so scary that some people would not enter the Trading Post. Thus, it was panelled over, and the image has never been seen since.

A photo in the *Telegraph Journal* of June 16, 1950, showed the painting of the Ug Wug at its unveiling. Based on this photo, reproduced here, you will have to decide for yourself if you would eat at the Trading Post if the huge, wall-sized image was uncovered.

The Reversing Falls were first lit when streams of light from an 8,000-candlepower airport lamp flooded the whirlpools and eddies at 10 P.M. on the night of August 16, 1928.

ROYAL ANTEDILUVIAN ORDER OF THE BUFFALO

On December 23, 1923, the *Saint John Globe* carried a notice that a branch of an English society with the aim of brother-hood and philanthropy was to be formed in Saint John following a meeting in the sergeant's mess of the local armories.

John Deering of the vessel RMS *Montcalm* was in the chair and explained the origin and objectives of the organization, which would be formed through the Grand Lodge of England. It is not a group whose work or whose presence is all that well know in Saint John, and the word "Antediluvian" is not one most know. Webster's says it means "old fashioned," while the Oxford Dictionary says it means "before the flood" and "utterly out of date." It is not a word that trips off the tongue, nor one that is spelled with ease. In fact, when the club was located on Union Street in the 1980s, the sign painter got the spelling wrong, but it remained uncorrected until the group moved in the early part of this century.

DO YOU RECALL?

The first government liquor store in Saint John was opened on September 6, 1927, at the corner of Charlotte and Princess Streets. "Hundreds of men, and some women, took advantage of the opening," according to a report in the *Evening Times Globe*.

SAINT JOHN CHRISTMAS TREE
TO ENGLAND

On December 8, 1949, on the fiftieth anniversary of sea trade between Saint John and Manchester, England, Mayor E. W. Patterson of Saint John visited the Manchester Line vessel *Manchester Trader* and presented Captain E. W. Raper with a thirty-foot fir tree to be erected in the home port of the vessel. Citizens of the city contributed Christmas tree ornaments and decorative electric lights so the tree would be ready to mark the festive season upon arrival in England. The mayor of Manchester sent a cable to Saint John saying, "On behalf of the citizens of Manchester I accept with warm thanks the Canadian Christmas tree offered by the citizens of Saint John...May the friendship and trading relationship between the two ports continue to flourish."

On December 24, the mayor of Saint John received a second cable from the mayor of Manchester stating that the Canadian trade commissioner presented the tree to Manchester. The note said that the tree had been revealed at the public ceremony the previous evening, and "the citizens of Manchester were deeply grateful to the citizens of Saint John for gifts and sends them Christmas and New Year wishes."

This seems to have been a one-time occurrence, and today there is no sea link between the two cities whatsoever.

STAR BUCK VALLEY—THE SKI HILL THAT NEVER CLOSED!

 Long before the Starbucks name was synonymous with coffee, there was a Star Buck Valley in Saint John, famed for skiing. In the days when the radio station CFBC gave regular updates on ski conditions at area hills, like Rockwood Park and Poley Mountain, it began to get calls reporting conditions at Star Buck Valley. Even when the two other hills would report no snow or closed conditions, Cecil Dark would report Star Buck Valley to be open and conditions as excellent. The disc jockey taking Cecil's calls, not being a ski enthusiast, simply reported what he was told. The listening public got curious about the location of Star Buck Valley and began calling in to see where it was. The next time Dark called in to report conditions, he was asked the whereabouts of Star Buck Valley and how it had such great snow conditions when other hills were closed. It was then they learned Dark was pulling their leg, as he revealed that Star Buck Valley was the old incinerator site off Milford Road, which everyone knew immediately as a steep precipice that would have been suicidal if used for skiing: skiers would have ended up in the turbulent waters of the Reversing Falls.

TELEVISION IN SAINT JOHN
— THE FIRST LOOK!

 Nine thousand people showed up at the Admiral Beatty Hotel at King's Square on Saturday, March 11, 1954, to catch the first glimpse of the programs that would be shown when CHSJ TV went on the air March 24. In co-operation with the Admiral Television Corporation, forty televisions were set up in the Georgian Ballroom of the city's leading hotel. Long before the official start of broadcast time at 2:00 p.m., a long line of curious citizens extended over a block from the hotel doors. Once the shows started the crowd moved speedily through the ballroom and passed by the TVs for a look at the first television broadcast in the Maritimes. The quality of the picture and sound drew many comments, and no doubt led to more than a few sales for Admiral Television. Local merchants were present, too, and were advertising sets available from $239 to $529, out of the range of many of the curious viewers who would be making $5–$10 a day.

The featured shows included:
- *Hopalong Cassidy*
- *CBC Concert Hour*
- *Holiday Ranch*
- newsreels
- cartoons

TUNNEL TO JOIN SAINT JOHN CENTRE WITH SAINT JOHN WEST

From 1882–1887, city engineer Hurd Peters was the chief proponent of a $750,000, 5-metre-wide tunnel under the Saint John harbour. There were various plans floated and all met with objections from the public, so the project was never undertaken.

As conceived by Peters, the tunnel would have entered the harbour at the foot of Princess Street at a 5 percent grade, follow the east side of the harbour to Reed's Point, then crossed to Rodney Wharf where it would have come up in Carleton. The distance would have been 1.6 kilometres, and the deepest point of the tunnel 30 metres under the harbour mud. Inside, there would have been train tracks, a roadway for horse and wagon, and a pedestrian sidewalk. Ladies from the west side, Peters claimed, could easily stroll through the electrically lighted tunnel for an afternoon of shopping on King Street and be home in time for supper. Though initial costs were a quarter-million dollars higher than a bridge, Peters pointed out that, unlike a bridge, there would be no maintenance costs once the tunnel was built. He also proposed a toll that would bring in $30,000 per year and pay the capital costs of the tunnel. Peters was basing his proposal on a successful tunnel built under the Thames in London at Southwark, but was unable to convince citizens on the merits of the idea. In 1889, it was decided a bridge was the better idea, but that, too, had it opponents. It took until 1968 before the bridge became a reality.

DID YOU KNOW?

The Saint John fire of June 20, 1877, destroyed two-thirds of the central portion of the city, up to 2,000 structures on 200 acres of land, which displaced some 13,000 persons. One-hundred-forty-six thousand dollars of financial assistance came from all over North America. By June 30, 1878, a year after the fire, out of the 3,027 people who had applied for relief, 2,771 were helped and 256 rejected. The financial loss of the fire has been estimated at 27 million, so the relief was miniscule in comparison to the loss.

WHAT HAPPENED TO THE IMPERIAL RELICS?

The Imperial Theatre marked its one hundredth year in 2013, but there was no sign of the relics found when the Keith Albee Company had undertaken the construction of the big playhouse a century ago. When the footing was being placed, bayonets, cannonballs, coins bearing dates as far back as 1818, as well as tools and utensils were dug up. At the time these were thought to be props from the productions of a former theatre, Lanergan's Lyceum, which had staged shows on the site. One show in particular, *The Relief of Lucknow*, was said to be responsible for many of the items, since the theatre management had used members of the 78th Highlanders Regiment, who happened to be stationed in the city at the time. The regiment was pressed into service to recreate the scene of "stirring Indian mutiny," as a report in the July 4, 1912, *Daily Telegraph* noted. The *Telegraph* continued that the Keith Albee Company had put the items in storage and would place them in a glass case for all to see when the theatre opened. No record exists showing that happened, and, if it did, the items have since been lost.

WHEN POLICE ENCOURAGED COASTING ON SAINT JOHN HILLS

 In November of 1933, Chief Slader of the Saint John Police Force announced that twelve Saint John hills would be set aside for safe sledding by the city's children. He urged parents to see that their children used only the hills named and promised that there would be a police presence on the hills from time to time. In addition, there had been stop signs placed at the crossroads of all the hills to ensure the children would have a safe sledding experience. The hills were:

East End:
- Cliff Street
- Richmond Street
- Prince Edward to St Patrick
- Brunswick Street
- Prince Edward to Erin
- St. David Street

South End:
- Carmarthan
- Mount Pleasant:
- Wright Street
- Parks Street

North End:
- Sheriff Street
- Harrison Street
- Acadia
- Chapel
- Victoria and Bridge Streets

No mention is made of Saint John West streets in the November 29, 1933, press release, though it is known that Miller's Hill on Watson was also designated a sliding hill, and that the chief once opened it for the winter by being the first to slide down its steep incline at breakneck speed.

A FIRST FOR FIBRE OPTICS IN CANADA

Fibre optics are standard today in the communication world, but it was only in August 1985 that the technology was used for the first time in a television transmission in Canada. This occurred when the opening ceremonies of the Canada Games, held in Saint John, were televised live across the county. NB Tel made the connection between their uptown office and the University of New Brunswick Canada Games Stadium by fibre optic cable. Rodney Graham was a young employee of the company at the time and recalls being proud of this accomplishment, one of many innovative ideas he saw the forward-thinkers of the company implement during his years with NB Tel.

JEWISH COMMUNITY'S FIRST SYNAGOGUE

The first synagogue east of Montreal was established in Saint John on January 11, 1899, when the Shaarei Zedek congregation built their synagogue on Carleton Street. Abraham Isaacs, the congregation's president, led the effort. The first in the Maritimes, the Jewish synagogue was reported on in the newspapers of Montreal and New York. Solomon and Alice Hart, the first Jewish immigrants to the city, arrived in Saint John in 1858, but numbers did not justify a three-hundred-seat synagogue until thirty-five years later. The congregation is still active today, and has also established the highly regarded Jewish Historical Museum at 91 Leinster Street adjacent to its present synagogue.

DO YOU RECALL?

The foot-high shaped-pine signs made by Murray
and Gregory? The last remaining sign was attached
to the warehouse of T. S Simms, which was demol-
ished in the winter of 2014. It is not known what
happened to the sign.

SIMMS AND CHURCHES

Simms—Brushes and Brooms and churches! The early success of
the big plant at Simms Corner was the result of the tireless work
of Thomas Stockwell Simms. He travelled widely to keep up with
trends in the broom and brush industry. He was as passionate
about his faith as about his business, and on one trip in 1907,
donated funds for a church to be built in Vizianagram, India. The
Simms Baptist Church, as it is known, is still open to this day.

The huge Simms Brush and Broom plant, which
featured 25,000 panes of glass as a distinct architectural feature, was torn down in 2014.

RELATED BOOKS IN THIS SERIES:

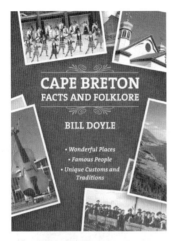

CAPE BRETON
FACTS AND FOLKLORE

BILL DOYLE

- Wonderful Places
- Famous People
- Unique Customs and
  Traditions

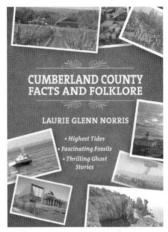

CUMBERLAND COUNTY
FACTS AND FOLKLORE

LAURIE GLENN NORRIS

- Highest Tides
- Fascinating Fossils
- Thrilling Ghost
  Stories

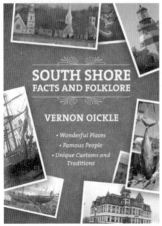

SOUTH SHORE
FACTS AND FOLKLORE

VERNON OICKLE

- Wonderful Places
- Famous People
- Unique Customs and
  Traditions

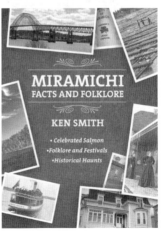

MIRAMICHI
FACTS AND FOLKLORE

KEN SMITH

- Celebrated Salmon
- Folklore and Festivals
- Historical Haunts